ADVANCE PRAISE

Missing Pieces is a powerful, raw, and deeply personal account of surviving the unspeakable horror of terrorism.

The author, Christi Scarpino, in 1977, at just twenty-one years of age, became a casualty of the Cold War, enduring a devastating FALN bombing in New York City that would become a part of her, ingrained in her for the rest of her life.

With unflinching honesty, Christi reveals how the trauma of that day and the ensuing investigation led to decades of pain, struggle, and PTSD, a reality of crime victims, terror survivors, and their families too often overlooked in the aftermath.

As someone whose father was murdered by the same FALN, I know firsthand how quickly the world moves on, leaving survivors and their families to pick up the shattered pieces alone and, in those days, without any government help.

Society labels survivors as "strong," assumes they are fine, and then forgets. But this memoir forces us to remember. It gives voice to those whose suffering lingers long after the headlines fade, exposing the deep and lasting scars of terrorism.

Missing Pieces is a compelling story of one woman's remarkable resilience. It also is an important historical document and a thought-provoking read. *Missing Pieces* challenges us to truly see the survivors, acknowledge their pain, and understand the heavy cost of terror beyond the immediate tragedy.

Joseph Connor
Author and Counter-Terror Advocate

As a fellow survivor of terrorism, *Missing Pieces* by Christiane Scarpino deeply resonated with me.

Her honest recounting of the emotional, physical, and mental aftermath of the bombing mirrored so many of my own experiences. Like Christiane, I, too, faced the unspoken weight of PTSD—flashbacks, anxiety, and the sense of disconnection from a world that couldn't understand what we had been through. Her raw depiction of navigating life and healing after trauma gave me a sense of solidarity that only a fellow survivor could understand. Christiane's ability to find resilience amidst such profound suffering truly inspires me. *Missing Pieces* not only offers a powerful window into the struggles we often endure in silence as survivors but also highlights the strength it takes to rebuild our lives. This memoir is a beacon for anyone trying to understand the long road to healing, and for fellow survivors, it is a reminder that we are not alone in this journey.

Elena Breese
Boston Marathon Bombing Survivor

Christi's *Missing Pieces* is a brave and brutally honest memoir that takes the reader through her struggle to learn about, identify, and battle through nearly fifty years of what is now known as PTSD.

She takes us on her difficult journey through post-traumatic stress disorder before she even knew what it was.

It's amazing how strikingly similar our journeys have been.

Christi was "blown up" in one of the early and lesser-known 1977 FALN terrorist bombings at the Mobil Oil Building in NYC. Her physical injuries were "minimal," but her psychological wounds would affect her deeply for the rest of her life. She doesn't understand it right away, and she doesn't know it will affect her for the rest of her life. Even those around her doubt her injuries and how serious they are for her. It cost her her career and relationships and denied her being able to do normal things with normal people again.

The symptoms she describes are common to people with PTSD as we now understand. It's incredible how many of us react to loud noises, loud crowds and other events similarly. We just can't do them.

As Christi begins to learn about this new diagnosis, PTSD, she begins to understand why she isn't normal and never will be again. However, she learns how to cope with it and live a happy life again.

She teaches us that we need to own our grief, not let it own us. She teaches us how to be patient with ourselves—and that's OK.

Take this journey with her and learn how she coped with her injuries. You'll find similar symptoms and learn her solutions that you may be able to use in your life. Find out if Christi, in the end, finds her missing pieces!

Tim Brown

Retired NYC Firefighter, First Responder, and 9/11 Survivor

Tim Brown is a retired New York City Fire Department/Office of Emergency Management firefighter who survived both tower collapses in NYC in 2001 and responded to the 1993 terrorist attacks on the World Trade Center, the 1995 Oklahoma City terrorist bombing, and the 1996 Centennial Olympic Park bombing. Tim is a U.S. Department of Defense subject matter expert in United States v. Khalid Sheikh Mohammed, et al., *the trial of five alleged al-Qaeda members for orchestrating and aiding the September 11, 2001, attacks,* also *known as* US v. KSM II.

In this poignant and inspiring memoir, the author recounts their journey of survival following a terrorist bombing in New York City in 1977 and her lifelong battle with PTSD.

Through raw and honest storytelling, she sheds light on the lasting impact of trauma and the resilience it takes to reclaim life. Central to this journey are her dogs, whose companionship became a lifeline.

From breeding and showing Boston Terriers in the 1980s to working with Nova Scotia Duck Tolling Retrievers (Tollers) for performance and service work, the author's bond with her dogs emerges as a profound source of healing and strength.

Her first Toller, Turner, provided life-changing support during her darkest moments, demonstrating the remarkable power of the human-animal connection.

This book is a testament to perseverance, the importance of mental health awareness, and the unconditional love that animals can bring. A compelling and heartfelt read.

Kathy Santo, IACP, CDT, CDTA, PDTI, CCAS
Dog Trainer, Author, and Owner of Kathy Santo
Dog Training kathsantodogtraining.com

I honestly could not put down *Missing Pieces*. The story is compelling, and I think it is going to be a tremendous help for people who have been through trauma. It's sad and uplifting at the same time. It's a story worth telling and I think Scarpino told it very well.

Tricia Thompson
Rhodesian Ridgeback breeder

Missing Pieces is a courageous memoir that gives hope to anyone who has been a victim of violence and suffers from PTSD. There is real comfort at the heart of this book to know it IS possible to work through trauma and find joy again.

Susan Lynch
Author of *Life After Kevin*

MISSING
PIECES

MISSING
PIECES

A Terrorist Attack Survivor's Memoir
of Trauma, Resilience, and Healing

CHRISTIANE SCARPINO

Press 49
4980 South Alma School Road
Suite 2-493
Chandler, Arizona 85248

FIRST EDITION

Library of Congress Control Number: 2025909457

ISBN (paperback): 978-1-953315-55-7
ISBN (eBook): 978-1-953315-56-4

SEL043000 SELF-HELP / Post-Traumatic Stress Disorder (PTSD)
HIS036000 HISTORY / United States / General
BIO026000 BIOGRAPHY & AUTOBIOGRAPHY / Memoirs

Interior and cover design by Medlar Publishing Solutions Pvt Ltd., India
Cover image courtesy of University of Virginia School of Law Special Collections & Archives and sketch artist Ida Libby Dengrove and used under the Creative Commons Attribution 4.0 International License

Printed in the United States of America

In honor of Charles Steinberg
January 6, 1951–August 3, 1977

To all victims of terrorism and their families,
may you find peace and justice.

TABLE OF CONTENTS

FOREWORD

It was 2018 when an unexpected, emotionally powerful email came through my website, forever connecting me with Christi Scarpino. The few years we have known each other have felt like decades, especially now, since reading her incredibly moving and deeply personal memoir, *Missing Pieces*.

In a sense, we have known each other since the 1970s, when our lives were forever changed and eventually intertwined by one common connection—a connection neither of us knew at the time, a connection we would give anything to get rid of, yet a connection that has shaped both our lives nonetheless.

That connection is terrorism, specifically FALN terrorism and its aftermath. The United States's war against terrorists is not new, nor is it limited to what we now see in the news—Islamic terrorists. Domestic terrorism has hit us for decades. The January 24, 1975, lunchtime bombing of Fraunces Tavern in lower Manhattan and the August 3, 1977, bombing of the Mobil Oil Building on the same day as an FALN threat caused the first evacuation of sixty thousand people from the World Trade Center in midtown Manhattan are just two of the many attacks of the twentieth century.

Our family was shattered that day at Fraunces in January '75 when my thirty-three-year-old father, Frank Connor, was one of four innocent men murdered in cold blood by the Marxist Puerto Rican Separatist Terrorists, the Armed Forces for National Liberation (FALN), on the very day we were to celebrate my ninth and brother's eleventh birthdays.

Similarly, and tragically, twenty-one-year-old Christi Scarpino's life was forever changed on a hot summer morning in August '77 when the same FALN terrorists bombed her office on the ground floor of the Mobil Oil Building. They murdered an innocent young man, Charles Steinberg, as Christi miraculously escaped with her life. Christi didn't know or feel like she was a hero that day, but she bravely confronted the terrorist and managed to keep the single fingerprint that unraveled the FALN conspiracy, doubtlessly saving the lives of other innocent Americans she would never know. Incredibly, I worked in the Mobil Oil Building three decades later, being reminded of the FALN's terror every morning in arriving at work.

The most prolific domestic terrorist group in US history, the FALN waged a decade-long war against the United States from 1974 to 1983, which included some 130 bombings and five murders. Between 1981 and 1983, sixteen core members of the FALN and Los Macheteros, a related group, were arrested, tried, convicted, and sentenced to appropriately long and well-deserved prison terms of between thirty-five and ninety years. Injustice ensued in 1999 and 2017, when the majority of the FALN terrorists were issued presidential clemency, further adding to the pain of their victims and families. Still, one terrorist remains at large as a guest of the Cuban regime.

In *Missing Pieces*, Christi captures the raw generational pain that terrorism inflicts on its victims and their loved ones, describing in detail the bombing that nearly took her life and the incredible yet tragic way her life was protected that day. This reluctant hero fearlessly confronts the unimaginable accusations and suspicions directed at her, the hero and victim, and the devastating triggering effects of post-traumatic stress disorder on not only the victim but also on her family, friends, loved ones, and even work colleagues.

Scarpino exhibits her inner bravery as she searches for truth in herself and the terrible situation thrust upon her. She ultimately confronts and overcomes the evil she endured beginning on that summer morning in 1977, knowing she is not alone, is no longer "broken," and has found her missing pieces.

Thank you, Christi, for your bravery in writing *Missing Pieces*. As you did in saving the fingerprint, the missing piece of evidence, you will save people you will never know.

Joseph Connor
Author and Counter-Terror Advocate
February 2025

INTRODUCTION: INVISIBLE

Over ten years, I have chipped away at writing this book. I'd write, get lost in thoughts, cry, and quit. It was tough to write about my trauma and see my emotional struggles in print. I wondered if anyone wanted to read my story...was it worth my time to write all this down? I didn't think something that happened to me in 1977 was relevant. However, when I realized the amount of violence, particularly terrorism, in today's world, I became aware that my story was more relevant than ever.

Life is full of challenges and emotions. We learn how to problem-solve and cope as we mature and gain more experiences. Most of us learn to navigate difficult circumstances, like the loss of a loved one, physical illness, or a fender bender. Family and friends are usually able to help. What we don't expect, and are never prepared for, is the occurrence of a severe traumatic event like one involving exposure to death, injury, sexual or physical abuse, or natural disasters. These are life-changing events, often with long-lasting effects of the trauma, known as post-traumatic stress disorder (PTSD).

My story begins in the late 1970s when I was twenty-one years old. As a young woman working in New York City, I was a victim (and survivor) and lead witness in a significant and historical act of terrorism—the one you'll soon read about—which changed the course of my life. After the event, I was barely able to function due to flashbacks, panic attacks, and a host of other symptoms. At that time, PTSD was not recognized as a disorder. It wasn't until 1980 that PTSD became a diagnosis, and even then, it was typically related to severe war-related anxiety. Because trauma-based mental illness was not yet recognized, few therapists had the expertise to work with my post-traumatic symptoms, and I didn't even know to call them that. (Neither did they at the time.) It took me four years and treatment from at least five therapists until I found someone who helped me cope with the symptoms of my trauma.

Generally speaking, the late '70s was also a time with little acceptance and understanding of mental illness. Society's lack of awareness of and compassion for any mental illness during that period caused me to hide my PTSD. Anyone could look at me and think that I was fine. From the outside, I had a great career, lots of friends, and was making my way in the world. The truth is I had to hide my mental health challenges in order to work and socialize.

If people knew, I might have lost my credibility and my job as a healthcare professional.

I hid my symptoms so well that other people did not know the "real me." Masking my symptoms gave me social acceptance. As I made myself invisible to others, I also lost touch with myself. My former self no longer existed. I did not recognize who I was and became detached from my emotions. I struggled with memory loss, and memory is a key component to identity.

Finding emotional support and services has been a challenge over the years. You will read about my quest to find solutions for my emotional pain during a time when community services for mental health were sparse. I have had to self-advocate for assistance, therapy, and ADA accommodations and learn to navigate my emotions. The services were simply not there for a woman struggling with PTSD. I am fortunate to be a strong-willed, determined person who is skilled at advocating for what I need, even going so far as to insist on being called Christiane, my post-1977 name, as opposed to Jane, the name I was given at birth. I have an intense drive to live, be happy, and thrive. However, I am aware that many people are not like me.

In recent years, there has been an increased awareness of mental illness, but understanding and support for people continue to be lacking. Every day, people's lives are impacted by gun violence, sexual assault, murder, suicide, and terrorism. The media consistently report the sensationalism of the event but never the lifelong effects on people's lives, such as PTSD.

Although public awareness of mental illness has increased, society has not yet embraced the lifelong effects of trauma. Unfortunately, those affected are frequently told they are being dramatic or just "need to get over it" and "move on." I wish it were that simple. As a result, people end up masking or hiding their mental health issues and become "invisible" like I was.

What happens to those who can't persevere and push against other people's negative attitudes or the "you survived, so get over it" attitude? What happens to those people who don't have an intrinsic drive to move ahead or want to but don't know where to begin? I hope my story will reach those people and give them incentives and directions to move forward and live their best lives—because they deserve it. If you are one of those people, my wish is that my book will help you find hope, strength, and the courage to take back your life.

PTSD and other mental health diagnoses need to be demystified so that people and their families can be transparent with their struggles and get the help they need. My memoir aims to instill a better understanding of PTSD so "regular people" like myself can be supported and get their needs met through therapy and ADA accommodations. Individuals, families, friends, and employers need to understand that PTSD responses may persist for decades following the traumatic event and that individuals may continue to need support for many years.

As you come with me in the pages ahead, realize that we all have the life force and strength within us. You may see parts of yourself in me and identify with my loss of self and need for closure. There may be some words, paragraphs, or even chapters that are triggering. Skip over those sections and move on. I have learned a lot on my path of recovery and healing from my trauma, and perhaps you will find some insights that will support you.

I have had many conversations with people who have experienced trauma different from mine, such as physical, emotional, or sexual abuse. I've come to realize that you can't compare traumas. Response to a traumatic event is an individual thing, and one type of trauma isn't necessarily worse than another. However, although the origin of trauma may be different, our responses may be manifested in similar ways in terms of behavioral symptoms, emotional responses, and patterns of thinking. Your personal story may differ from mine, but we likely share many of the same symptoms that can hinder our ability to function. As you read my story, may you realize that you are not alone in your struggle to function and that there is hope.

CHAPTER 1

SUMMER IN THE CITY

It was the summer of 1977, and at twenty-one, I had just graduated with my bachelor's degree from Douglass College of Rutgers University in New Jersey. I spent the summer in Mount Vernon, New York, before starting my graduate school journey at Purdue University in Indiana. I was breaking out of my sheltered upbringing to become an independent woman ready to build a future. I felt like a butterfly that was about to emerge from the cocoon. The only problem was that I was living with my parents for the summer, and they wanted to keep the silk threads tightly wrapped around my cocoon to control my independence. So, I focused on working, saving money, and planning my future career.

Living in metropolitan New York in the 1970s made a young person grow up fast. It made you rough and hardened to reality in order to survive. The environment in New York City and the suburbs was more violent and dangerous than ever before. Shootings, stabbings, bombings, riots, blackouts, murders, muggings, drug deals, and prostitution were all daily occurrences. Left-wing terrorist groups such as the Weather Underground, the New World Liberation Front, and the Symbionese Liberation Army left so many bombs that bombings were accepted as a way of life. Heroin addicts having bad trips in the streets were also considered "normal." Even at twenty-one years old, my parents still warned me to stay out of Hartley Park, which was a hub for drug activity.

That July of 1977, an extensive heat wave and a twenty-five-hour blackout extended through NYC and the suburbs. The darkness was filled with the sounds of people shrieking in the streets and shattering glass from the looting of storefronts, as well as the vision of heavy smoke and flames from burning buildings. It was frightening, and I stayed inside to protect myself. And sometime that month (and the next), the Son of Sam, the .44 Caliber Killer, was at large. This serial killer was stalking young couples on dates and killing them. Many of us did not go out on dates while the manhunt was on.

There was so much violence in the '70s that New Yorkers became hardened to it. Daily headlines didn't even phase us. It was just another day of life in the city. I became numb to it like most other people. It was the only way to get through the day.

In 2024, it seems like we have returned to the '70s with an increase in domestic terrorism, and nobody seems to care.

Terrorist acts are soon forgotten. Victims and their families are left to cope on their own. We haven't learned a thing from history.

Despite it all, I loved New York.

What I thought would be an enjoyable summer in my favorite city of New York turned out to be the summer that would change the rest of my life.

That summer of 1977, I worked as the receptionist in the employment office at Mobil Oil Corporation on Forty-Second Street in NYC. This was my third summer as an intern at Mobil. I greeted people who entered the office looking for employment and then processed their applications. I loved this job because it was interesting; I met people with different backgrounds and experiences beyond my limited world as a student. I also got along great with my co-workers. This was the first time I felt like I was part of the group at a job. I felt like I was valued as a colleague and a friend. We got together after work, ran together, and even spent some weekends at a beach house in Long Island.

My father also worked at Mobil as manager of ship dispatching. Supposedly, he had no influence on my getting the job. I did my best to stay separate from my father and be my own person. My father tried to be influential in all avenues of my life. That made working at Mobil challenging, but I think I made my mark without his help. I did everything possible to be Jane Scarpino rather than Captain Scarpino's daughter. On the other hand, my mother encouraged my individuality and let me make my own decisions. She was available if I wanted to talk about something and always provided the structure I needed for work- or school-related tasks.

My mother's voice reminded me it was time to start the day every morning. "Jane, it's time to get up for work. You have a train to catch." I'd jump out of bed and carefully select a color-coordinated outfit, along with high heels or platform shoes. At four feet eleven, I felt I needed additional height to look more mature.

On Wednesdays, I would take my running clothes with me to go running with my colleagues, Donna and Dianne, after work. We were preparing for a corporate relay race through Central Park as part of the Mobil Oil Corporation team. We were only one week away from the race, which would take place on August 3.

On this last Wednesday before the race, I had no time for breakfast. I walked the mile to the train station in Fleetwood for the Harlem line to Grand Central Station. After I purchased my ticket, I waited on the platform for the 7:57 a.m. train to arrive. I could hear the brakes squeal as the train approached, and I cautiously stepped into the train and found a place on the hard, green seats.

As my body rocked back and forth with the clickity clack of the train, I carefully put on my makeup without a smudge, then settled into people-watching and looking out the window. I could see kids playing in the streets and women in apartment houses hanging their clothes on a line many stories above the ground. The sky was yellowish-brown from the pollution, but occasionally, you would see patches of blue with fluffy white clouds.

My mind drifted to last night's dinner conversation with my father.

My father, a stout man, balding, and in his early sixties, was very opinionated. He always served his opinions with dinner and cocktails. He would make himself a scotch straight up and sit at the circular wooden table in the dining room. Mom sat at the twelve o'clock position, me at three, and Dad at six. Last night, he started the conversation by taking a big slurp of scotch. He leaned toward me and, using his sweetest tone of voice, he said, "Jane Margaret, I hope you are thinking about what you want to do with your life."

I leaned back a little in my chair, reacting to the strong smell of his scotch. "I'm going to Purdue to become a speech-language pathologist," I reminded him, as I had many times in past conversations.

He paused momentarily to swirl his drink, inspecting the contents, which were half gone. "Well," he said in a disdaining tone, "You aren't going to make much money, and I want my daughter to be successful. You should be a doctor."

I closed my eyes and sighed, "Dad, I don't want to spend my life in school. I want to be a speech-language pathologist, work in a hospital, and live my life. I don't want to be a doctor."

He set his glass down on the table with a clang. "Well," he said emphatically. "That's not what I want for you. You need to be important and successful. There's no two ways about it."

I gritted my teeth and stared at my plate of iceberg lettuce, waiting for him to smack his lips to start the next phase of the conversation that I already knew by heart.

He remained silent for five minutes as he finished his scotch.

Then there it was—the lip smack and the "Don't forget you need to get married. Your mother and I don't have any grandkids yet. Your brothers and sister haven't come through, so it's up to you. Marry a nice Italian boy and have kids."

I rolled my eyes and continued eating my lettuce in an effort to ignore him.

I felt so conflicted.

On the one hand, I felt like my father was telling me I needed to be married to have purpose. On the other hand, my brother, Jon, told me I needed to pursue a career to have purpose. *"Get your graduate degree and follow your dreams. Don't get married and throw away your education. That would be a waste,"* Jon said. My sister, Karin, and my brother, Guy, didn't make any comments about this, but they were also more career-oriented. Even though my considerably older siblings no longer lived at home, they always looked out for me, their baby sister. It was like having three additional parents. I was always worried about pleasing my father and siblings to avoid verbal backlash if my decisions didn't match their expectations. It was time for me to be honest with myself.

It was one of those conversations in which I was reminded how much I wanted to choose a career over being a wife. I had a very different perspective about my identity now that I had been to four years of college. Four years of college education that embraced women's liberation made me an independent thinker. I had become quite outspoken about my needs and desires, which did not always sit well with my parents. My father still tried to dictate every aspect of my life, but now I pushed back.

What do I really want for my life? What is most import-ant to me? Do I really care what they think now that I'm a grown-up?

I swallowed hard before I told my father what I thought.

I put down my fork and cleared my throat. "Well, Mr. No-Two-Ways, I am not going to please you. I don't want to be a doctor, and I'm not even considering having a family. I'm not even dating anybody. I can't be a dedicated career woman and a stay-at-home mom. So, right now I choose career first as a speech-language pathologist."

We sat in silence for the rest of the meal. My stomach was in knots because I knew my father disapproved of my choices, but I no longer thought he was able to make the right choices for me. I was a young, independent woman now who wanted to make my own decisions, learn from my own mistakes, and manage my own life.

The train hit a bumpy part of the track that jolted me out of my seat and snapped me out of my daydreaming. It was 8:20 a.m.

I heard the conductor shout, "Grand Central Station. Last stop. Grand Central."

The screech of the tires along the metal rails was piercing as the train slowed to a stop. I rose quickly, ready to throw elbows to get off the train if needed.

I carefully stepped onto the platform to prevent myself from twisting my ankle in my platform shoes. It was only a seven-minute walk to my office at 150 East Forty-Second Street, but I had learned to walk fast like a New Yorker. I looked straight ahead, ignoring the beggars on my left and stepping over the homeless people sleeping on the sidewalk.

My shoes' hard, slapping noise as my feet hit the ground signaled that I was walking intently and on a mission. My first mission of the day was to get my breakfast. I walked the final block to the deli on the corner of Park Avenue and East Forty-Second Street, which was conveniently located at the end of the long lobby of the Mobil Oil Building. I went in and placed my order.

"I'll have my usual toasted bagel with cream cheese and a large black coffee to go, please," I said to the guy at the counter. I paid for my order and then walked out the side door into the lobby of the Mobil building. My office was just a short distance down the hallway on the left.

I opened the double glass doors to our office and turned left to enter the reception area. It was a straight shot to my desk and the filing cabinet behind it. The office design was an open concept with a twenty-foot ceiling.

When someone walked into the reception area, they would first see my desk. To the left was a waiting area with tables and chairs where people could fill out their applications. Behind the waiting area were three small rooms that were used to give typing and shorthand tests. There was a coat rack in the left corner of the waiting area, which was seldom used. To the right of the reception desk were four offices (that were more like cubicles) that were separated by five-foot partitions instead of real walls. You had to negotiate around a potted philodendron taller than me (which meant it was at least five feet tall) to get to the cubicles like a roundabout.

Heading around the plant, exit one on the right was Donna's office, exit two was Luanne, exit three was my boss, Dorothy, and exit four was Dianne. Dorothy and Luanne bordered the front side of the office, which was an enormous plate glass window that faced East Forty-Second Street. Most of the time, the blinds were down, but the world outside could see us when they were up.

I plopped my breakfast on my desk in the reception area and unlocked the filing cabinet behind me. My job was to greet all applicants, review their résumés, have them complete an application, give a brief interview, and administer typing and shorthand tests. I was the first person applicants would see as they entered the office. We kept the employment applications and résumés from potential candidates in the filing cabinet.

After completing the process, I would write a summary of the applicant's strengths and weaknesses on the back of the application. I decided whether the application was filed or forwarded to the appropriate department for review. I kept a daily log of applicants, the disposition of their applications (forwarded or filed away), and their ethnicities.

We were an Equal Opportunity Employer (EOE), and the company needed to consider ethnicity when hiring. My boss reminded me of two cardinal rules: 1. Record all EOE data so the company records would be accurate, and 2. Never let a person leave with their application. We needed all applications to support our EOE data and in case of inquiries from Social Security or the unemployment office.

I learned to gracefully take applications from people who wanted to leave with them to get more information about references, dates, or previous employment. A qualified applicant always has the necessary information with them. I think one of the reasons I was hired back a third summer was that I was diligent about following the rules and keeping accurate data.

Back at my desk, I was ready to start the day. I prepared my applicant record-keeping forms for the day to begin my data-keeping. Next, I had to check the three small rooms where applicants were given typing and shorthand tests. I straightened up the rooms and turned on the IBM Selectric typewriters so they would be ready for applicants to demonstrate their typing skills. I checked the coat racks to see if anything needed to go in our lost and found bin and to ensure the reception area was spotless.

I glanced up at the clock above the doorway to the middle room and saw that it was 8:45, so I had fifteen minutes to eat my breakfast before my official starting time for work. I mentally prepared myself for my day as I finished my bagel.

I loved my job at Mobil. It wasn't that difficult, and it could be quite colorful. Located on Forty-Second Street and close to Grand Central Station, it was a convenient location for interesting characters to come in out of the heat or rain or just come in to talk. I enjoyed all the interactions, even the strange ones.

Some people dressed very professionally for a job interview, and others were barely dressed, looking like they just rolled out of bed. Some people didn't speak English, and some talked to themselves.

A man came in several times and claimed he was Jesus Christ. He wore a dark robe, had shoulder-length dark hair, and a beard. I found him entertaining and almost comical, but I also wondered if he needed mental health services. Although he seemed convinced he was Jesus, he hadn't questioned why Jesus would need to apply for a job at Mobil.

"Are there any jobs?" the young, bearded man would ask.

"Yes," I'd reply. "Please fill out this application."

He'd write a few minutes, then hand me his partially completed paperwork. He would always write "Jesus" in the name section, and for job choice, he would write "Anything."

I'd review his application with him and ask questions to fill in the blanks.

"Last name?"

He'd respond, "Jesus doesn't have a last name. It's just Jesus."

"Address?"

"Jesus doesn't have an address. Jesus is everywhere."

"Thank you for your time. I'll keep your application on file."

I'd then write a quick summary of our interaction and file his application with all his previous ones.

Some days were filled with interesting applicants, and other days, the applicants were just regular people looking for a job.

By ten a.m., nothing out of the ordinary had happened. People came in to apply, and I ran through my routine with them. And, per usual, we had our mid-morning coffee break. This was usually timed with recruiters from employment agencies popping in to inquire about job vacancies for their clients.

My favorite recruiters were Ivan Gearson and Charles Steinberg from Viva Employment Agency. I thought they were good-looking men with great personalities. They were probably in their twenties, not much different in age than me. I knew Charles was married. I didn't know about Ivan.

They frequently stopped by to see what employment opportunities we had available and if they had any suitable candidates for us. Their visits were as much a social visit as a professional visit; they broke the monotony of the office on any particular day. My fellow employees and I would gather around as Charles and Ivan told jokes about the recruiting industry and teased us for drinking too much coffee. Charles, in particular, was very outgoing and social. Charles was also a talented musician who played in rock bands on Long Island. Clearly, he used his charm as a performer to establish personal connections with potential employers to benefit his clients.

The remainder of my day was spent reviewing employment applications, interviewing potential candidates, and administering tests for typing and shorthand.

At 4:45, I headed to Grand Central Station to take the thirty-seven-minute train ride home, mentally rehashing the day as I walked. Once on the train, I elevated my feet as much as possible. I still had the mile walk home from the train and planned to go for a six-mile run. I typically ran to the north side of town, near the expensive homes and into safer neighborhoods.

A couple of hours later, after returning home from my run and showering, it was time for dinner with my parents. Sometimes, this was lovely. Other times, I couldn't wait for the meal to be over. It all depended on what topics of conversation came up. I was hoping we wouldn't have a repeat of last night's marriage conversation.

There were regular dinner conversations and rituals that I could no longer tolerate, such as stereotypical gender roles within the home, which were also illustrated at this particular dinner. My father thought it was a woman's role to do all the housework and chores, cook all the meals, and wait on men. He expected my mother and me to stop whatever we were doing the moment he came home and devote all our time and attention to him. I was not on board with this.

My mom made spaghetti and meatballs, salad, and homemade bread for dinner, which was one of my dad's favorite meals. After mopping up the spaghetti sauce with a piece of bread, he pushed his plate in front of me, indicating that he was finished and ready for the next course.

"Dad," I whispered, "I will clear your plate when I finish eating my spaghetti."

Gruffly, he proclaimed, "I walked to and from the train station and worked hard all day. I'm hungry and tired. Bring me my coffee and dessert."

I sat up, and in the most assertive voice I could muster, I responded, "Dad, I walked to and from the *same* train station, worked an eight-hour day, and then ran six miles."

I took in another swift breath and continued.

"I'm not your servant. Get your own coffee and dessert."

I tucked my chin and stared at my plate, wondering how that would go over.

My mother's jaw dropped as my father got up, cleared his dirty plate, and brought in dessert for all three of us, which was the first time I had ever seen him serve us instead. I am sure my mother was shocked that my father backed down and did not argue with me. I also think she was envious that I could stand up to my father when she could not.

I exhaled a little and then enjoyed the sweet relief that came with every dinner after that. He never again asked me to get him his dessert or clear his plate. I am sure I earned more of my father's respect that night. I was becoming the independent, assertive woman I needed to be for a successful career ahead.

This was a critical turning point for me, even though it was as simple as rejecting my father's order to get his dessert.

I learned at this moment that words could have a magical effect of getting you what you want or turning down what you don't want. I would never be afraid to speak my mind again. There is power in self-advocacy, even if it can fall on those who choose not to hear or see you. Little did I know how much I would rely on this skill throughout the rest of my life.

I was growing up mentally and beginning to figure myself out. I was starting to verbalize what I wanted to do and how I wanted to live my life, which was in opposition to the gender roles that my parents embodied. I wouldn't let anyone tell me how to live my life and what was best for me. I was taking control of my life. The captain's daughter would sail her own ship no matter the weather on the horizon.

CHAPTER 2

AUGUST 3, 1977

August 3, 1977, started as a beautiful, sunny day. The commute to work was normal. As I swayed back and forth with the lazy movement of the train, I felt excited about what the day had in store for me.

We were running the corporate relay race after work in Central Park. I wondered if this race would be a ticket to a full-time job offer at Mobil. In my naive twenty-one-year-old way of thinking, I somehow thought being a part of an after-work company-affiliated event would lead to a job offer. I loved my job and the people I worked with, and maybe working here was the "right" move, even if it didn't make my heart sing. Maybe my dad was right about making a lot of money or having a stable income.

Truthfully, what I dreamed of was being a concert violinist. Ever since I was a young child, I had been interested in playing a musical instrument. My mother and sister played piano, but the piano didn't suit me because of my tiny hands accompanying my petite body. When I was in fourth grade, my elementary school offered private music lessons. My parents agreed I could select an instrument and they would pay for the rental and lessons. My first choice was a clarinet, but there were none available. My second choice was a saxophone, but there were none available either.

I was told that only violins were left to rent, so that became my instrument. As it turned out, fate came into play as I became a talented violinist and played in several local orchestras, including the Westchester Youth Symphony and the Bermuda Philharmonic. When I went to college in 1973, I double-majored in music and speech-language pathology. After a few music courses, I realized that I would need to become a music teacher to have a consistent income. This was not appealing, so I decided to drop my music major and major only in speech-language pathology. At the time, I continued playing violin as a side hobby but stopped playing altogether in 1980. There have been times since that I became motivated to play again, but it was no longer pleasurable. Looking back, I believe that part of me—the talented musician—drifted away, along with the rest of me, in the aftermath of August 3, 1977.

Pursuing speech pathology was actually my mother's idea. Unlike my father, my mother wanted me to do something I loved. She knew I loved to talk and that I also wanted to help people. She was sure I would feel happy and fulfilled assisting others to communicate when they could not. I trusted my mother's judgment, and she turned out to be right, as I enthusiastically helped people communicate for forty-five years.

As I sat on the train, my head was filled with thoughts about my future. *"I hope I have made the right career choice. Speech-language pathology might be right, but Mom suggested it. Maybe I should be open to other career paths. Maybe I would be happier working in the corporate world in NYC. Maybe Mobil will offer me a full-time position."*

I controlled my doubt with a more positive thought: *"Nothing is going to ruin my day."*

"Grand Central. Grand Central," the conductor announced, and I found myself again leaving my thoughts behind to begin my hustle to work. As I stood in the crowd to get off the train, I brushed the wrinkles from my tan bell-bottom pants and unfastened the top button on my shirt so my necklace would show.

My necklace was the first piece of jewelry I bought for myself. It was a gold chain with a diamond chip and ruby teardrop hanging below it. After my first summer working at Mobil, I bought it from a real jeweler (not a department store) with my hard-earned money. It represented my newly found independence and financial freedom and gave me a taste of becoming my own person. It would later become my talisman as a symbol of strength, protection, and a reminder that I was still alive.

The crowd behind me pushed me out of the train, and I took a few quick initial steps onto the pavement in my wooden platform shoes with the macrame beaded tops. I realized the train was a few minutes late, so I decided to walk faster and skip breakfast at the deli. I was almost jogging, hugging my bag of running attire close to my body. I could already feel a blister forming on my right foot, and the workday had not even begun.

As I walked into the Mobil building, I noticed that the sky had suddenly clouded over, and it was starting to rain, a drastic shift in the weather since stepping off the train just minutes earlier. *I hope the rain doesn't continue all day so the race is canceled...On the other hand, inclement weather can make for an interesting workday.* We had had some very interesting people apply for jobs simply to get out of the rain.

I opened the double glass doors into the office at 8:40, which was still twenty minutes before we were officially opened for business. That morning, I parked myself at my desk and was getting organized when the door opened. At 8:50, the first applicant of the day walked in. The door was unlocked, so I did not turn her away.

"Good morning," I said to the petite woman drenched by the rain. She was holding a small, black, collapsible umbrella. I welcomed her in and invited her to my desk.

"I want to apply for a job," she said in a heavy accent, which seemed Spanish. My guess was it was Puerto Rican because she sounded like my college roommates from Puerto Rico. I also took college courses in linguistics and dialects. I paid close attention to her accent because I thought it would help me identify her ethnicity for equal opportunity employer (EOE) data.

"What type of job are you looking for?"

"Clerical," she replied as she nervously fumbled with her umbrella.

I gave her an application and asked that she fill it out.

She wasn't much bigger than me, which sparked my interest and curiosity as I am used to people being much taller than me. She had unkempt blonde hair and was wearing a straw hat and sunglasses. *Why would someone wear a straw hat and sunglasses when it's raining?*

My sixth sense was telling me this woman was eccentric at best, given her costume-like appearance, hurried demeanor, and nervousness. Her dry, straw-like blonde hair clashed with her darker skin, and I could tell it was a cheap wig. She was obviously in a hurry as she fumbled with the application, the black umbrella, and her purse. She gripped the umbrella and purse tight to her body as she rushed over to the table in the corner of the room. I wondered what her life was like and what else she had planned for the day.

She sat at a table by the coat rack, removed her sunglasses, and worked on her application. After a few minutes, she stood and headed toward the double doors to leave. "Can I help you?" I politely asked as I approached her.

"I need to take this home to get more information," she said.

"Well, you can't take that out of the office," I replied adamantly as I moved between her and the doors. She held the application close to her chest as she tried to push by me. I dug my feet into the carpet, making my ankles wobble in my four-inch heels.

We were now standing an inch apart, eye to eye. Her dark brown eyes had an intensity that penetrated through me, making me shudder. Her voice became very high-pitched, and I could hear her respirations as she loudly exclaimed, "I am going to make a phone call in the lobby, and I will be right back."

She put her hand on my chest as if to keep me away, her dark eyes piercing through me, and started moving towards the doors. She waved her application in the air and shouted, "I told you I will be right back!"

"I told you I will hold it for you," I blurted as I snatched the application from her hands. She flung open one of the glass doors and ran out.

In that moment, I missed a critical detail.

She left behind her umbrella.

Our altercation was sufficiently loud for my boss Dorothy to come to see if I needed help, but by the time she arrived, the woman was gone, and I was standing rigid and shaking. The sweat from my hands left marks on the application.

"Are you OK, Jane?" she asked.

"I think so," I replied. "There was something really odd about that woman, but I didn't let her take her application out of the office."

"You are good at following the rules, so we have accurate employment data," said my boss. "Take a few minutes to collect yourself. The office is quiet at the moment."

I took the woman's application and put it on my desk to process.

"Sandra Peters" was the name on her application. *Sandra Peters*, I thought, *is not a qualified applicant.*

I would process her as a Puerto Rican female for our EOE statistics. Little did I know that Sandra Peter's application would be a crucial piece of evidence someday.

It was around 9:30 when my coworker, Donna, announced she was going to the deli. "Do you want anything from the deli, Jane?"

"I'll take a large black coffee and a toasted bagel. I didn't have time for breakfast today."

About ten minutes after Donna slipped out, Ivan and Charles stopped in.

"Hey Jane, is Donna around?" Charles asked.

"She just stepped out to get coffee, but she'll be back soon," I replied.

"We'll just wait until she comes back," Charles indicated.

Around 9:45 a.m., Donna walked right by me, carrying a Styrofoam tray holding coffee and my bagel. Because I was busy with paperwork, I did not see her come in. She buzzed me using the interoffice phone on her desk. I put down my pen and picked up the receiver. "Jane, come get your coffee and bagel. I'll see Charles and Ivan after I brief you on the day."

I put the receiver down and walked up to Charles and Ivan, standing a few feet from my desk. "I need to talk to Donna for a second, and then she'll be ready to see you," I told them.

I left the men standing at my desk as I turned and walked back to Donna's cubicle for my coffee.

I took one step....

and then another step....

and then ......

no more steps.

A powerful force surged from behind, thrusting me into the air.

I felt like my body was being squeezed into nothingness.

There was nothing, and I was transported into a realm between the conscious and unconscious.

Maybe I was dead. I wasn't sure.

I was searching for any evidence of my reality.

My sensations could not be described.

Sickly.

Surreal.

Floating.

Overload.

Pressure.

Pain.

Silence.

CHAPTER 3

CHAOS

I don't know how long I had been lying on the floor. I felt numb and paralyzed. Confused, isolated, and helpless. My head felt like it was being compressed to the point of my brain emerging from my forehead. How bizarre that I felt external and internal pressure. Surely, this must mean my brain is damaged. The experience of my brain being squeezed from my head would replay over and over again in my future.

What happened?

Where am I?

Am I dreaming?

Am I dead?

As I opened my eyes, I saw that my surroundings were unfamiliar. My eyes were burning from the dense gray smoke, which was also burning in my lungs.

What is this painful pressure on my head and chest?

As I gasped for breath, I could see pieces of the ceiling tiles hanging down, smoking and burning. There were chunks of plaster and dust everywhere.

The smell....oh, the putrid smell. The smell of gunpowder. The smell of burning furniture, ceiling, walls. Perhaps the putrid smell I couldn't identify was the smell of burning flesh.

I now understood the phrase *deadly silence*. I was in the middle of an unidentifiable mess of fire and smoke. There was no sound. Maybe the pressure around my head affected my hearing. I was just lying there, scared. This must be the end of my life.

As I searched the space for clues, I noticed one familiar sight—the giant philodendron. My head was next to the white planter it sat in, and as I looked up, I could see its vibrant green leaves through the smoke and debris around me. There it was, tall and healthy-looking with its giant leaves still intact. It was still there. I could see it. I could touch it. That was the only thing I recognized, and it gave me comfort.

How bizarre that this resilient plant in the center of the room shielded me from the devastation of what used to be the Mobil employment office. I would visualize its green, leafy presence for many years as a reminder that I survived as it did.

I propped myself up a little to see if I could identify anything else. I could see fragments of what used to be the walls splattered with red. My stomach turned as I realized that this was blood.

A slight breeze touched my forehead as I noticed the large plate glass window shattered, and the office was open to the street. This silent, stagnant scene was interrupted by the appearance of several men jumping through what used to be the wall to our office. Dressed in dark uniforms and wearing helmets, the men ran into the area. Maybe they were here to save us. These men were later identified as the NYPD Bomb Squad. My last memory of being inside the office was them running towards me.

My next recollection was being in the middle of Forty-Second Street with my co-workers.

Donna, Dianne, Luanne, Dorothy, and I huddled in a circle in the pouring rain. I don't remember how we all got there and ended up together. The men from the bomb squad must have taken us through the broken plate-glass window that overlooked Forty-Second Street.

Did they get me off the floor and take me outside? Did they carry me or walk me through the broken plate glass window to Forty-Second Street? Did they talk to me? I have no memory of any of this.

There was glass covering the sidewalk and the street.

Traffic was stopped.

There were people everywhere, meandering about.

I reached for my necklace and rubbed the ruby teardrop between my index finger and thumb. It reassured me that I was alive, although I wondered if it still could have been a dream.

The group of us held each other tight but did not say much. We all seemed to be in shock, frightened, and trying to figure out what happened. One of us asked about Charles and Ivan, but nobody answered. Our question was brushed aside.

We were told that a threat had been made of a bomb in the lobby earlier that morning. The lobby had been checked by the bomb squad and was cleared for no explosives.

Nobody thought to check the offices, such as ours, that were located *off* the lobby. Nobody thought it was important to notify employees of a bomb threat.

What became clear in that moment was that a bomb went off in our office. I didn't know what that meant. How could a real bomb find its way into an employment office? Who would even do such a thing? What else could have blown out the plate glass window onto Forty-Second Street? If it hadn't been for that window, we probably would have all died from the pressure of the explosion. The most important question I found asking myself was how did we survive it?

At some point, as we huddled on the street, I worried about my new Adidas. I needed my running shoes, T-shirt, and running shorts for the race after work. *What is wrong with me*? I thought. *I didn't grab my running shoes as I left the building*. I was sure I would be using them that afternoon in Central Park.

Why, during a crisis, do we focus on unimportant details? On some level, I was aware of the level of destruction and mayhem in what used to be the employment office. Yet, I was compelled to enter a room with blood-stained walls to get a pair of running shoes. Ludicrous. I must have been in shock and was not thinking clearly.

For many years, I was sure I re-entered the building to look for my shoes but couldn't find them. I'm sure I did not go back in because the police would have stopped me.

My coworkers and I stood outside together, wondering what we should do next until the NYPD officers told us we had to go back inside the Mobil Building. I have no idea how long we were out there. Minutes? An hour? No clue. I only have sporadic memories of the day and no concept of time. That was the beginning of my amnesia.

"Okay, ladies. You all need to go up to the medical department to get checked," one of the officers said. *Go to the medical department? That's wild! Who thinks it is a good idea to go back into a building that was just bombed? There are ambulances outside. Aren't they there to take us to the hospital to get checked?*

Despite feeling like my head would explode, I thought more rationally about safety and medical evaluations than the NYPD. However, when I expressed my concerns out loud, nobody listened.

My colleagues and I were escorted back into the Mobil building.

The five of us were walked to the elevator by several police officers, and then we went up to the medical department on the sixth floor. As we stepped into the medical office, we were greeted by a nurse.

"Are any of you hurt?" she asked, smiling patronizingly. It was clear that she had no idea of the magnitude of the destruction downstairs. "Is anyone bleeding? Burned? Feeling sick?" I knew I wasn't bleeding or burned, but my mental state prohibited me from deciding if I was otherwise OK.

If this traumatic event were to happen today, we would have been taken to the hospital, checked for a concussion, and maybe have an MRI or CT scan. But in 1977, we were evaluated by a nurse who asked if we were feeling OK and checked us for wounds and burns. She didn't even listen to my heart or take my blood pressure.

When it was ascertained that none of us had a scratch or a burn or were limping, we were all cleared to return to work. RETURN TO WORK. How ludicrous to expect us to return to the office and fulfill our job responsibilities. Was it that the nurse did not realize there was no office to return to? We were expected to walk right back into the danger zone—one that could have killed us all. Did the company feel that our job responsibilities were more important than our lives? It's sad to think that processing employment applications was more important than our health and safety.

I wish I could say the concept of work productivity being valued more than health and safety was limited to this one experience. However, throughout my career, over the next forty years, I would experience bomb threats or threats of violence (school shooters) in the workplace three more times. In those situations, we were evacuated, the threats were "checked," and we were told to return to work. Because of my experience with the Mobil bombing, I could never walk back into any building that had just had a threat of violence. I'd go home and was docked a day's pay because

I left work without cause. I never understood the lack of concern for safety exhibited by administrators and how they never seemed to take the threats of violence seriously. I was perceived as being overreactive.

Back in the medical office, I took a minute to collect myself back in the office after the nurse told us we could leave. I looked down at my shoes and noticed red stains and debris stuck in the macrame. My shoes were ruined, and my feet were dirty. But I was going to have to get through the day like that. I wondered if Charles and Ivan went back to work, if they also had dirt on their shoes, or if they were hurt.

My father was at work that day in the Mobil building, managing the dispatch of oil tankers. I started to get concerned that my father would be worried if he found out the employment office was bombed, so I asked the nurse if I could use her office phone to call him. She handed me the phone, and I dialed his extension.

"Captain Scarpino here," he said.

"Dad, it's Jane…There was a bomb in the office… I'm OK. I'm in medical…" The nurse began to signal to me to hang up the phone. "I can't talk. I have to hang up…" Her face was growing graver by the second. "See you later," I said, not paying attention to what he said in response. I put the receiver back in the cradle and looked at the nurse.

"There was another bomb threat," she said, her voice shaking. She finally appeared to understand the gravity of the situation. "The entire Mobil building is being evacuated. We need to leave right now and take the stairs."

We found the door that read "exit" to the stairwell and opened it. The stairwell was already crowded with people moving so slowly that I thought we'd never get down the six flights of stairs. We pushed and wiggled our way into the masses so we could make our way to safety. The sound of my wooden platform shoes on the metal stairs echoed, and my feet ached from the repeated hard contact on the steps. The movement down the stairs was painfully slow. So many people squished on the stairwell trying to move faster created the effect of actually moving slower. I felt like I was waddling down the stairs. With anticipation of another explosion, I wanted to fly right over the top of these six flights of people. My right foot was killing me as the macrame top rubbed open the blister on my toe that I got earlier that day.

My heart was pounding from the fear of a second bomb going off. *If we go down these stairs any slower, we may never get out of the building,* I thought. *What if another bomb goes off, and we're stuck in the stairwell? What if another bomb goes off IN the stairwell?* It seemed like it took hours to get down the steep stairs to the main floor, and as we entered the lobby, I wondered if it was still pouring or if we could go outside without getting drenched.

I don't recall walking out of the building, but we made it.

My office colleagues and I were again in the street, surrounded by police. The street was mobbed with many more people than before. When we were evacuated after the explosion, it was just the five of us from the employment office, the police, and bystanders. This time, the entire building of employees was evacuated....about three thousand more people. The sight of ambulances and the sounds of sirens and people yelling made me realize the gravity of our situation. *Oh great*, I thought. *It's pouring rain. No umbrella. No shelter.* The rain was so fierce that it bounced off the sidewalk, causing little bursts of steam. My clothes were drenched, and my airy, boho top was sticking to my back. We had to stay together, and we had to stay with the police. I just wanted to go home. I kept hearing the words—*suspects, bombing, police, bomb squad, FALN*—words a twenty-one-year-old college student could not process after surviving an explosion.

"We can't stay in front of this building," the police told us. "You ladies from the employment office need to stay together, and we'll take you to another building where you will be safe." I wondered why we were being separated from all the other evacuated employees.

I began to panic, and my thoughts began to reel.

Why wouldn't we be safe standing in the street with the police?

I thought we were safe. I thought that since we were out of the building and away from any bombs, we were out of danger.

I squeezed my necklace with my right hand as the police hurriedly escorted us down Third Avenue to *another* Mobil corporate office building.

Well, this is a really stupid idea.

If there are more bomb threats, why are we going into another Mobil building?

Why are the police so interested in us?

How can I trust the police who say we're safe, but apparently, we're not?

Why can't I just catch the train home?

The five of us sat in the other Mobil corporate office building, staring at one another in silence. Even though we didn't speak with words, our eyes shared the same sentiment of frustration from not knowing what the hell was going on. No one was filling us in. No one seemed to notice or care that we were drenched and cold in the frigid, air-conditioned room. I twisted my shirt to wring out some of the water, hoping that would make me feel more comfortable. My waist-length, blonde hair was in soggy clumps down my back, dripping into the waistband of my pants.

It seemed like we were sitting there alone for hours when one policeman finally graced us with his presence. "There's been a bomb threat on this building. We have to go NOW."

Donna and I exchanged glances and knew we would not put up with another evacuation. It seemed like the police did not know what they were doing, and we were just being moved like pieces on a chessboard.

"This is the third time we're being evacuated today," Donna asserted. "Nobody has told us anything. Enough is enough. We want to know what is going on."

"Well," said the officer in a matter-of-fact tone. "The FALN has been calling bomb threats all over the city.

Buildings all over New York are being evacuated. The city is paralyzed."

Who were they? What did they want?

We weren't given the details at that moment. I later learned that the Armed Forces of National Liberation (or Fuerzas Armadas de Liberación Nacional Puertoriqueña in Spanish, FALN) took responsibility for the explosion at the Mobil building and several other buildings in NYC that day. This terrorist group had been setting bombs in Manhattan, Chicago, Newark, and Washington since 1974 and was the focus of grand jury investigations.

On August 3, 1977, a typewritten note was left in Central Park at the base of the statue of José Martí, a Cuban revolutionary. The note called the bombings "just a warning" to "multinational corporations" that "explore and exploit our national resources" and are part of "Yanki Imperialism."

The note asked for the freeing of five Puerto Rican nationalists who were jailed in the 1950s for shooting several members of the House of Representatives and attempting an assassination of President Harry S. Truman. The note also stated that they wanted to call an end to the grand jury investigations. The note was signed "FALN Central Command."

The FALN made several phone calls on the morning of August 3 with bomb threats to the NYPD, *Eyewitness News*, and the *New York Post*. The FALN provided a list of at least seventeen office buildings where bombs were allegedly set. Among those listed were the Mobil Oil Building on 150 East Forty-Second Street, the Chase Bank branch office at 410 Park Avenue, and 1270 Avenue of the Americas, where there were several Latin American consulates, the World Trade Center Towers, and the Empire State Building. Police were dispatched to investigate the buildings mentioned, which placed an even tighter strain on a police department that was already spread thin with the Son of Sam investigation.

In that moment, speaking with the police officer about being evacuated again, even without all the context I would learn later, I understood that we were a small part of a more significant terrorist attack on NYC, but I still didn't understand why we were being moved from place to place and why we just couldn't go home. I was a very naive young woman who always followed the rules and was never involved with law enforcement. I was a "good girl," so there was no reason to detain me. I just wanted to go home, eat, and take a nap. The NYPD had a different agenda.

The five of us were escorted out of that building and were taken to the office of the New York Police Department. Or maybe it was the FBI. It's difficult to remember, as time was blurry in those first few hours and for many years after that. Over the next three years, I got to visit the sterile offices of the FBI and NYPD so many times that the officers and interrogations blended into one gigantic pain in the butt.

We all sat in metal folding chairs in a straight line in an empty, sterile-looking room. Our energy was depleted, and our wet bodies stuck to the metal chairs. Serious-looking men walked in and out of the room, their footsteps echoing as they moved.

As we sat together side-by-side, we exchanged looks of exhaustion and the desire to be done with these officers, who all looked and acted like the same annoying person. Very little information was given to us about what happened and why we were being detained. I knew we had been involved in a terrorist attack by a Puerto Rican terrorist group. I didn't understand what that meant then. I had never heard of the word *terrorism* before. I just wanted to go home.

My stomach was growling, and my mouth was parched. I never got my morning coffee and bagel, and it was long past lunchtime—that much I knew. I stared at the red stains on my shoes and finally had time to wonder whose blood it was.

CHAPTER 4

SLIPPING AWAY

The blood on my shoes...Nobody else noticed enough to question me about it. Not then, and not since. I'm the only person who ever knew blood was on my shoes that day. But there were other questions—lots of questions. Questions that continued to come at me for the next thirty-four months, leading to a federal trial. The questions began sometime in the afternoon that day of August 3 when a tall man in blue pants, white shirt, and glasses gestured for me to come over to him, pulling me away from my coworkers. However, they, too, would have their time being escorted to separate rooms to be questioned.

"Follow me," he said in a flat, unfeeling voice as he led me into a small room with no windows.

He pointed to a metal chair in front of a small table and told me to sit. I plopped myself down in my wrinkled, damp clothes, wishing I looked and felt better. He sat across from me with a cup of coffee and a bulky meat sandwich.

"I have some questions for you," he stated, then took his first bite. The sandwich, unfortunately, was for him, not me.

Throughout the day, there had been no questions about our physical or emotional well-being nor consideration for our physical or emotional needs. We had gone all day without food or drink, evacuation after evacuation—almost ten hours. I was exhausted from walking, answering questions, and not having my questions answered.

We had been sitting in damp or dripping wet clothes for several hours, enduring questioning, were fingerprinted, and then asked the same questions repeatedly, perhaps with a different officer. It was hard to tell at that point because they all looked and acted the same, as if we were all somehow involved in the planting of the bomb.

"First of all, tell me your name and why you were in the Mobil Oil employment office this morning."

"My name is Jane Scarpino, and I am the receptionist for the employment office."

"Did anyone come in to apply for a job this morning?" he asked.

I then described my interaction with the petite blonde woman with the straw hat and sunglasses.

I thought I had sufficiently described the scene when he looked over the rim of his glasses and said, "Are you sure that is what happened, Miss Scarpino?"

I had been asked, "Are you sure that's what happened?" so many times that, by that point, I was no longer sure what had happened. I'd been questioned so many times that now I questioned myself. Were my coworkers being asked if they were sure, too?

"Yes, I'm sure," I responded.

He chewed vigorously on his sandwich while he asked me the same questions in different ways several times. After most questions, he asked if I was "sure" of my answer. As he spoke, I could see pieces of sandwich roll around in his mouth, causing me to feel nauseous and simultaneously notice my own hunger. By then, I would have missed breakfast and lunch and, apparently, now would miss dinner. I hadn't had a sip of water all day. I was tired, hungry, frustrated, and didn't know why I was still there.

He finished his sandwich and sipped coffee, cleaning his teeth with his tongue afterward. "That's all for now," he said. "We'll talk again later."

Later? How much later?

Before he managed to leave the room, I barked at him. "Can I call my parents?"

"No phone calls," he sharply replied.

The way he had spoken to me throughout our time together was just another example of the lack of concern and compassion the officers had for me or the other women who survived the explosion, not to mention our family members who, at that point, didn't know anything about our well-being.

My parents had no idea where I was—if I was caught up in another bombing or even if I was alive. Knowing my father, he had either worked himself into a panic attack or was popping nitroglycerin tabs like candy due to his heart condition. However, I could only guess my parents' thoughts because they never spoke about their emotions. In my family, discussing emotions was a sign of weakness.

I had been interrogated for several hours, and the clock on the wall now read 8:00 p.m. He escorted me back to the room, and I rejoined my coworkers. All five of us were together again, sitting silently and looking at the four walls. One of the officers told us that there were more questions for us, and then we could go home. *What else could they possibly ask?* I wondered.

"I have nothing more to say," I snapped at the officer. "I have told you everything I know. In fact, I have told you the same story several times." My usual quiet demeanor transformed into a mighty roar as my voice became louder with each successive word. My intense, quivering voice surprised both me and my coworkers as I shouted, "I need something to eat and drink! I am so hungry I can't even think." I shifted my weight in the chair and folded my arms. "I am not talking again until I have something to eat." I thought, *If you want me to help you with your investigation, you need to treat me like a human being, not a piece of garbage.*

Around nine o'clock, we were still sitting together, waiting for more interrogation and permission to go home. An officer came in and finally gave us some dry sandwiches and Coke. I hated Coke, but I drank it anyway. At that moment, I realized that my words had some bargaining power. I could say "no," and nobody could make me talk anymore. The police could move me around, make me sit in a chair, and ask me a million questions, but they couldn't make me talk if I didn't want to. I took some comfort in knowing I had a little control by just keeping my mouth shut. For someone who loves to talk, this was a new slant on effective communication.

It was close to midnight by the time they let us go, and I have no memory of the time between receiving the sandwiches and getting to leave. I imagine it was more of the same barrage of questioning that filled the remaining time. When they finally decided we could leave, I wondered how I would get home since I knew the trains stopped running and I had no money for a cab. My personal belongings were not retrieved from the office and most likely had been destroyed by the explosion. We still were not allowed to make any phone calls, so I couldn't call my parents to drive into the city to pick me up. Was I being released onto the streets of NYC in the middle of the night to find my way home?

To my surprise, a black limousine was parked at the curb, waiting to take me home. I was told that the president of Mobil Oil Corporation sent the limousine.

When I got home, I expected that my parents would have been crying for joy to see me alive. My mother was asleep, but my father was sitting in the living room. In reality, my father was angry that I got home so late and that he did not know where I was for the past twenty-four hours. He thought I should have called him again later in the day, but I explained I had no access to a phone while being interrogated. It bothered me that he was angry, but it wasn't my fault. I didn't decide to come home after midnight because

I was having too much fun being interrogated. We didn't discuss what happened that day or how we felt. After all, that would have meant we were weak.

I did not go to work the next day or the day after. In fact, I never went back to work in the Mobil building. I do not know what happened in my coworkers' lives after the bombing. Contacting them never crossed my mind because I was hyper-focused on my own problems.

On August 4, the day after the Mobil Oil bombing, the *New York Times* headline read "100,000 Leave New York Offices as Bomb Threats Disrupt City: Blasts Kill One and Hurt Seven. Puerto Rican Terror Group Takes the Responsibility." My stomach felt sick, and I wanted to put the paper down. But I forced myself to read the article's contents, hoping to find out exactly what had happened in our office the day before.

The newspaper article explained that a bomb exploded in the employment office of Mobil Oil Corporation, instantly killing Charles Steinberg and injuring several others. I did not know that Charles was dead until that moment. This was the first time I experienced death.

My stomach was in knots, reading the article, trying to piece together what had happened.

The article stated that Charles Steinberg and his coworker, Ivan Gerson, from the Viva Employment Agency, were waiting at the reception desk. They were there to see if there were any job openings for their applicants when the explosion occurred about five feet from them.

How did The New York Times *know that they were five feet away from the bomb? They weren't there....but I was. The reception desk was MY desk. I was standing next to Charles and Ivan until I walked away to get my coffee. Bomb? Where was the bomb?*

According to the article, the bomb was inside an umbrella, which was hung on a coat rack. I suddenly had a vision of Sandra Peters nervously fingering the black umbrella that she was holding. She left the umbrella on the coat rack and then hurried to leave.

My heart was racing, and I couldn't catch my breath as my eyes darted across the page. I could no longer focus on reading complete sentences. Instead, short phrases stabbed my eyes, and I felt the pressure squeezing my head.

"Metal door bent in half."

"Plate glass window shattered onto Forty-Second Street."

"Holes in the ceiling."

"Furniture jutting from the walls."

"Splattered blood on the walls and curtains."

"Receptionist's desk was shattered."

For a moment, I felt like I was back in the office. I saw the blood on the walls and curtains. I saw the blood on my shoes. I saw the holes in the ceiling and glass everywhere. The room was unrecognizable.

The article mentioned that there were several people on the floor, bloodied and moaning.

Was I one of those people? What happened next?

Mayor Beame called this "An outrageous act of terrorism" in the article. I didn't understand what this meant. I did understand that I had lived through something horrific.

I took deep breaths and closed my eyes, reassuring myself I was home and OK. I noticed that I was breathing easier now that I was clutching my lucky necklace.

After a few minutes, my breathing and heart rate returned to normal, and I could concentrate again. I continued to read about how all the employees and applicants who were in the Mobil employment office were interrogated by the FBI and NYPD that day to determine if they were involved in the bombing. Fingerprints were found on an application left that morning. One fingerprint matched mine—no wonder they were interested in me, though it was obvious why my fingerprint was on the application. I was the one who always handed the applications to the applicants, no matter who they were.

The FBI Laboratory eventually identified the other fingerprint as belonging to Marie Haydée Beltrán Torres, age twenty-two. She was the wife of Carlos Alberto Torres, twenty-five, who was a leader in the FALN. He was wanted for the FALN bombing of Fraunces Tavern in NYC in 1975.

Marie Torres aka Sandra Peters. I had a face-to-face confrontation with a terrorist. A terrorist with a bomb in her umbrella. A terrorist intent on blowing up my office, my colleagues, and me. And she nearly succeeded.

I have literally survived to tell this tale.

The problem with the article, or rather society at the time, was that it was just another headline about violence that disrupted the entire city. In fact, it was just another headline to be long forgotten except by those who were innocently made a part of this nightmare. After that day, there were a few short articles about the event, but most news focused on the Son of Sam investigation. The terror of August 3 was soon forgotten by most of NYC. Yet, while it was just another headline for everyone else, it was a terror that has lived in my breath and bones for over forty years.

I don't know exactly what I did on August 4 after reading the article. I was home with my parents, and they didn't say much. I imagine I was supposed to return to the NYPD the next day. Maybe I did.

If I did, it was one of many dates with the NYPD and FBI where I had to repeat the story over and over again. For the next thirty-four months, every time I was hauled away for questioning, I would answer the same questions asked by several different people for hours on end. It always ended with, "Are you sure this is the way it happened, Miss Scarpino?" Interrogation upon interrogation. *Do they think I am lying or stupid?* I wondered. A few questions would have been fine. But the final dig was, "Are you sure you're sure?" They dug at me until I questioned my own story. They dug at me until I broke down and cried. Then, I was called uncooperative because I physically couldn't answer any more questions.

Eventually, I had interrogation nightmares.

To this day, I am nervous and sometimes agitated when someone asks me a lot of questions. Questions in job interviews, lines of questions to get approval to judge dog breeds (a passion I developed later in life), and even questions from my personal trainer increase my anxiety, sometimes causing me to lose eye contact and stop speaking. The question, "Are you sure?" causes me to shut down. I once quit an interview to get the approval to judge sporting dog breeds because this question was asked too many times. I politely said, "I'm sorry. I can't do this anymore." I collected my things and walked out of the interview room. It was too complicated and embarrassing to explain, and the result was that I did not pursue approval for any other breeds because of my anxiety.

Truthfully, the day after the bombing was the first day Jane, the social, self-confident, budding career woman, began disappearing, entering into a whole new, mosaic world. My life, my identity—it was now like looking through broken glass, trying to recreate a picture that would always have cracks. I'd have to decide if I could live with the cracks and see the picture as broken or thrive in the face of the cracks and see it as purposeful, beautiful, and strong.

Sometime during the week after the bombing, I felt like I was slipping away from reality. I was unable to eat or sleep. I would wake up in the middle of the night screaming. I would cry uncontrollably.

My father's words reverberated with me.

"You have no reason to feel like this. After all, you are alive."

"You need to get over this and move on. It's over."

"You have a lot to be thankful for. Don't be weak. Get ahold of yourself."

I agreed my life was spared, but I also knew that I had no control over the nausea and the nightmares. I felt so guilty and so ashamed that I had no control over my reactions, and even worse was that I was being weak. Every night, I would dream so vividly that I would wake up thinking I was lying next to the philodendron and could smell gunpowder. Sometimes, I would even feel pressure around my entire body like I was enveloped by a snake that was trying to squeeze out my guts. Sometimes, I would see myself stepping over Charles's body.

I don't know if I can rise above this was a frequent thought I replayed in those earliest days. Eventually, I did. It took years, but I made it "above." Still, at that time in the late 1970s, in those first days and weeks, I was reliving the bombing regularly. Nobody told me I had post-traumatic stress disorder (PTSD) until thirty-seven years after the bombing.

PTSD was not recognized at that time unless you were a soldier or veteran who was in combat. Civilians didn't get PTSD; hence, there were either no services for people like me or therapists didn't know how to work with people like me. I described myself as "broken" or "I'm fragments of glass scattered on the table with missing pieces." Nobody gave me any help, and therapists didn't want to talk about it. Most of the therapists that I went to wanted to talk about my childhood or my relationship with my father. Now, I'm not saying that I didn't need to work through some of my family issues. Still, I needed somebody to give me strategies to get through the nightmares, the vomiting, the lack of appetite, and waking up every day thinking I was lying on the floor in the Mobil employment office. Time and time again, my mental illness was recognized as being overly dramatic or not necessary. After all, I had lived through a bombing, so I must just get over it because that is what strong people do.

I heard my father's words, but I couldn't embrace them. The physical event was over, but I was not over it. I was different. I had changed. I didn't understand it, couldn't control it, and pieces of "Jane" were missing. The trauma of surviving a terrorist explosion became part of me, and it never went away.

I tried to follow my father's advice and push it out of my conscious mind, but it hibernated in my body. I am living proof that the hibernation of trauma inside your body can cause physical ailments and emotional issues. I experienced digestive problems, difficulty swallowing, and physical pain for years. Anxiety and depression became part of daily living.

My parents and I never talked about what August 3 was like for me. We never spoke about my feelings of loss and despair, my confusion, or my nightmares. My mother hounded me because I wasn't eating enough. My father hounded me because I was too emotional. They expected me to cope and snap back into normal. None of us knew then that it would take years before the "normal" Jane reappeared. None of us knew that my parents would never live to see her again; they passed away before I truly found my way back to myself.

My father's way of helping me to cope was to take me away from it all. A few days after the bombing, he put me on a plane to Bermuda, my happy place, where I stayed for two weeks. My parents and I lived there for my sophomore and junior years of high school while my father set up a ship dispatching office for Mobil. It's always been a beautiful place that made me feel comfortable, happy, and grounded.

After arriving there and spending some time walking on the beach, I realized I felt like a different person. The happy Jane who ran on the pink sand beaches wasn't there. The different Jane sat on the prickly coral formations in solitude and wished for the ocean to wash her troubles away. The sound of the waves and the salt air did not release me from nightmares and negative thoughts. After two weeks of solitude, I felt less confident and wasn't thinking straight. Maybe I'd feel more like myself in NYC. I got on a plane back to LaGuardia Airport.

✶ ✶ ✶

When I arrived home, I quickly realized wishes don't always come true.

I exited the plane and entered the terminal where my mother was waiting to bring me home. She was my mode of transportation since I didn't have a driver's license. I depended on my mother, public transit, and my bicycle to get from one place to another.

"Hello, my darling daughter," she said in her usual sweet tone. "Your chariot awaits," referring to the family vehicle, a baby blue Mustang. "Let's go get your luggage."

We found the flight's carousel in the baggage claim area and waited patiently until we saw my oversized blue suitcase. As I pulled it off the carousel, I noticed the zipper was partially undone. I quickly zipped it up and dragged it down the walkway to the terminal exit. (In those days, suitcases did not have wheels).

In the middle of the walkway, I heard someone yell, "Miss. Oh, Miss! STOP! STOP right there!" A glance told me that the person yelling was a security officer. I wasn't sure he was talking to me, and if he was, I was hopeful that he would help me navigate the terminal with my heavy suitcase. I stopped and turned to look at him.

"Are you Jane Scarpino?"

"Yes," I said, puzzled that he knew my name.

The man took a big step forward, grabbed my suitcase from me and threw it on the floor. As my mother and I stood in disbelief, he dumped the contents on the floor. He pawed through the contents, picking up items and tossing them aside.

"What's in here?" he said, holding up my bottle of shampoo.

"Shampoo," I replied as he opened the container and inspected it. Next, he found a jar of homemade loquat jam made by a Bermudian friend.

"And what do you have here?" he asked.

"That's homemade loquat jam," I stated as calmly as possible.

"Never heard of it," he said as he opened the jar and sniffed it. He took the jam, the shampoo, and any other containers he could find. He never introduced himself or revealed the purpose of the search. I was pretty sure it was just a random search for drugs because I was a young woman with blonde hair down to her butt that looked like a hippie freak. Wishful thinking on my part.

As I knelt on the floor to gather my belongings and stuff them back into my suitcase, I noticed two other official-looking men holding handcuffs.

"Jane Scarpino," said one of the men who turned out to be a United States marshal. "You need to come with us. The FBI needs to speak with you."

My relaxing vacation came to a screeching halt as I was put in handcuffs and escorted out of the airport, eventually taken to the FBI headquarters in NYC. My mother watched in disbelief. She couldn't do anything but gather my things and take them with her. The ocean had not washed away my troubles. My troubles were just beginning.

I was considered a fugitive since I left the country as a suspect in a crime under investigation. I recall someone saying to me, "You are a prime suspect until proven otherwise...You may have connections."

The fact that I had Puerto Rican roommates in college was a possible connection.

The fact that I was in the Mobil Office the morning of the bombing made me a suspect.

The fact that my fingerprints were on everything in that office made me a suspect.

The fact that I left the country and wasn't available for their investigation made me a suspect *and* a flight risk.

In reality, I was simply an innocent young woman whose father tried to protect her by sending her on vacation. My father's efforts to protect me turned me into a fugitive, and ironically, the system made me feel like a criminal.

My thoughts overwhelmed me. *I didn't do this. I was just in the wrong place at the wrong time.* In fact, I was so overwhelmed by the turn of events that I wished I had died in the bombing. If I had died, they couldn't torment me by dumping my suitcase contents on the floor, taking away my loquat jam, publicly embarrassing me at a national airport, putting me in handcuffs, and considering me a primary suspect and fugitive of the state.

There could have been one day or many days of interrogation. It became a blur of repeated questions and checking to see if I was "sure" of my answers. During one of those days, I had to look through piles of photos of people to see if I recognized anyone.

As I turned the pages of a thick book filled with photos of people wanted by the FBI, it dawned on me that dangerous people were everywhere. I thought I recognized several people from their photographs, and the thought that terrorists and killers walked among us every day sent chills down my spine. Some I thought I saw on the train ride to work. Some I remembered came into the employment office, and some I thought I remembered from Rutgers University.

The FBI agents seemed interested in the fact that I had two Puerto Rican roommates in college. They were from Jersey City, which just happened to be a place where FALN members were living under assumed names. Of course,

I didn't know that at the time, but it made the FBI examine the possibility that I had connections with Puerto Rican terrorists.

Quick lesson learned: *The FBI and NYPD treat suspected criminals and fugitives like dirt.* To hell with respecting people's basic human rights for privacy. To hell with understanding a person's basic need for food and water. To hell with the concept of innocent until proven guilty.

I started to question my place in the world and what I did to be treated so poorly. I was a good girl. I never broke the rules. I tried to please people. I wanted to do the right thing. Now, I realize that the FALN Mobil bombing was a significant historical event in which I played an important part. Yet, I was treated like I didn't matter. The truth is, my actions gave the FBI the evidence to link a specific member of the FALN, Marie Torres, to the bombing. The FALN had been responsible for several bombings, but this was the first time there was hard evidence that a specific member of the FALN was responsible for a bombing. I did not realize this until 2018.

I figured out that sometimes bad shit happens to good people. I was a good person who was gaining control over her life. I certainly didn't deserve this shit, and I wondered how I got into this mess with the FBI and NYPD. I certainly wasn't a terrorist. I didn't have a violent bone in my body. I didn't intend to be a fugitive.

I'm not sure exactly when, but at some point, the authorities changed my status from prime suspect to prime witness and from fugitive to flight risk. But I wasn't treated any better. Suspect or witness, fugitive or flight risk—I was treated the same.

*   *   *

I had only two weeks left before heading to graduate school out of state and hoped that my leaving New York for education wouldn't make things worse with the FBI and NYPD. I felt conflicted about leaving or staying in New York because of the flight risk issue. Graduate school seemed like my best option, even though apathy about my studies had snuck in. In fact, indifference was my predominant attitude about most things, including running, being with friends, and even talking. What happened to the "old" Jane, who was gregarious, motivated, and confident? My identity was gone. I tried my best to move on, according to my father's wishes, but I felt stuck in nothingness.

One of my last evenings at home before departing for school, my mom and I sat together sipping on a glass of Gallo red wine, as we frequently did when my father came home late from work. I decided to talk to her about how I was feeling differently since the bombing.

"Mom, I don't feel like Jane anymore."

"Well, who do you feel like?"

"I don't know. Not Jane. Not Jane Margaret. Why did you name me Jane Margaret?"

"Well, my darling daughter," she explained. "Your father and I agreed that if you were a boy, you'd be named Harold after him, and if you were a girl, your name would be Jane after me. Margaret is your grandmother Scarpino's first name."

I took a few big sips of wine as my brain tried to process the irony of my name selection. My father's name was Harold, but everyone called him Skip because he hated Harold. My mother's real name was Florence Jane, but since she hated Florence, everyone called her Jane. My maternal grandmother's name was Margaret; however, she called herself Marguerite because she hated Margaret, but the family called her Lady. Was I even named after my mother and grandmother?

This conversation with Mom was fascinating...my family members used other names because they didn't like their birth names. Maybe I should do that!

"So...Mom, if you didn't name me Jane, what name would you have chosen? Did you have a favorite name you were saving for another girl?"

"Well, my dear," she sighed. "I wanted to name you Christiane, but your father wouldn't have it."

At that moment, I became Christiane. From that point on, I told everyone my name was Christi. However, memories of Jane lingered. The FBI and NYPD officers who needed me for their investigation called me Jane. Everyone who knew me before the bombing, including my family, called me Jane. I started to insist that everyone call me Christi, which people (especially family) found difficult. Now, I allow people who knew me before 1977 to call me Jane, but post-1977 friends (and some family) call me Christi.

At that moment in 1977, the persona of Jane was dead.

CHAPTER 5

BUTTER THIEF

A t the end of August, I flew to West Lafayette, Indiana, to start my graduate studies in speech-language pathology at Purdue University. I was fortunate to assume a position as a residence counselor in one of the dorms, which covered my tuition and meals. I was very excited about having new learning situations and meeting new people but also relieved to be far away from the trauma of New York City, where the terrorists were. I thought moving to the Midwest would keep me far enough away from the NYPD and FBI for further questioning. Nothing was further from the truth.

I was at Purdue to learn and to study, and I had the concentration of a gnat. Studying used to be easy, and I had an incredible photographic memory. That was gone now. I could no longer visualize what I read on a page. I could no longer remember what was said in lectures like in undergrad. I took copious notes during class, used the cassette tape recorder for lectures, re-wrote my notes, and then typed my notes. Even after doing all that, sometimes my head would be void of information. I had trouble talking in class. If a professor asked me to explain a concept, my mind would go blank, and I could not answer. The student who got A's without trying hard was gone. (My inability to remember new information was most likely due to a brain injury from the explosion, resulting in amnesia, but I didn't know that at the time. People weren't assessed or treated for a closed head injury in the '70s.) My lack of concentration, confusion, and poor memory frustrated me. I felt stupid.

How did I become so stupid?

Why can't I remember anything?

Everything used to be so easy.

Now, everything is a struggle, including tasks of daily living.

Why can't I get out of bed when it rains?

How do I find a way to break through the terror in my head?

Why can't I be normal?

I reacted to so many ordinary things: straw hats, rain, pocketbooks, umbrellas, stairways, police officers, high heels, sunglasses. Seeing these things made me freeze in terror. I could not move my body as I held my breath until the object was out of sight. Every day, I would see one or more of these things, and every day, I would freeze in panic. If it was a rainy day, I could not get out of bed. I continued to wake up in the middle of the night in a heavy sweat, thinking about Charles, smelling smoke, and feeling pressure around me like I was being compressed. Sometimes, I would scream because I saw blood on the walls of my bedroom. It looked and felt so real, even though I knew it wasn't.

I did my best to complete my studies and my resident counseling responsibilities despite my limited memory, nightmares, and panic attacks. Two things got me through each day: my excessive running and studying. I had stopped running for a couple of months immediately after the bombing, but I missed the sense of calm and being grounded. I needed to run; the more I ran, the better I felt.

I filled every available moment of the day with one of those tasks because it kept the replay of the bombing out of my head. I ran ten miles daily during the week and twenty miles on Saturdays. It was hypervigilance—another sign of PTSD I later discovered. Hypervigilance was my therapy for a long time. Maybe I was running away from myself or the flashbacks and intrusive thoughts.

Somehow, I found my way to the graduate counseling center. Janet was the graduate student assigned to be my therapist as part of her clinical practicum. This was my first experience with any kind of therapy. I wanted to work on my fearful reactions to objects that Janet called "triggers." Janet used a behavioral therapy technique called systematic desensitization in our sessions to teach me to relax in the presence of anxiety-provoking stimuli or triggers—the rain, straw hats, sunglasses, staircases, and umbrellas. She also taught me to use progressive relaxation to reduce my anxiety by tensing and relaxing specific muscle groups.

Our sessions were held in a small room in the psychology department on campus. When you entered the room, there was a comfortable brown recliner that I always sat in.

Janet sat in the wooden chair directly across from me. Next to her was a small, rectangular table where she placed her tape recorder, a pad of paper, and a pencil. Behind her was a one-way mirror so her clinical supervisor could observe our session.

Janet started most of our sessions like this:

"Christi, I want you to lean back and melt into the soft chair. Close your eyes and notice that your body is feeling heavy."

I positioned myself farther back in the chair, allowing my head to sink into the fabric.

"Christi, imagine you are sitting on the beach in Bermuda, the place you love the most. The scene is so peaceful, and you feel very relaxed with the soft breeze, the scent of the ocean air, and the gentle sound of the waves rolling in."

My eyes, although closed, fluttered a little as I pictured waves breaking into foamy white water as they touched the pink sand.

"Memorize that feeling. Remember it."

I could feel my shoulders soften as I imagined hearing the waves and smelling the salt air.

"You are very relaxed."

My thoughts focused on the warmth of the sun and the softness of the breeze during a few minutes of silence.

"I will count to five, and you take a deep breath in and slowly let the air out with each number. Ready?"

My mind came back into the room as Janet started to count.

"One."

I took a breath in and slowly exhaled.

"Two."

My breath slowly filled my lungs, and then I emptied them.

"Three."

I could feel my diaphragm rise and fall with the third inhalation and exhalation.

"Four."

My breaths were getting smoother and deeper.

"Five."

I touched my stomach to feel it slowly rise and fall synchronously with my breathing.

"There. Your breathing is relaxed; your entire body is relaxed. Memorize that feeling of relaxation. Hold onto it."

I sat in silence for a minute or two to allow my body to absorb my relaxed state.

Next, Janet would introduce one of my triggers.

"Christi, now imagine it is a very sunny day, and you are walking to class. On your way, you see a woman wearing sunglasses."

With my eyes still closed, I pictured a female student wearing sunglasses walking towards me.

"Check in with yourself. Notice any areas of tension in your body as you notice the sunglasses. Tighten the muscles in that area where you feel tense."

I could feel the tension in my jaw, my neck, and my shoulders. I pressed my lips tightly together and raised my shoulders towards my ears.

"Make them tighter."

"TIGHTER."

"TIGHTER."

I clenched my teeth so hard that my lips parted, and I felt pain in my neck. I continued to contract my neck and shoulder muscles until my breathing became very shallow.

"Continue looking at the woman's sunglasses, and now, let go of that tension. And relax."

I let my shoulders drop while letting my jaw open as I pictured the sunglasses.

"As I count to five, breathe deeply and find that good feeling of relaxation you remember."

While Janet repeated the counting sequence, I would find myself breathing more deeply and letting go of tension. She would always end the session with a visualization of the beach in Bermuda.

From my work with Janet, I could go out in the rain, use a stairway, and be in the presence of straw hats and sunglasses. She made a relaxation tape for me, which I practiced daily. Her cassette tape got me through many days. The semester ended, and Janet could no longer be my therapist because she had completed her clinical practicum.

I did not mesh with the next girl who was assigned to me, and the university clinic decided that I should go to a professional therapist in the community. I must have been a basket case.

I don't remember much about the professional therapist other than I didn't think she helped me much. She prescribed an antidepressant called Imipramine, which I took for a couple of years. Therapy ended when the funds ran out. I don't know who paid for it, but they stopped paying.

After therapy ended, I managed to get through the day using Janet's relaxation tapes and running. Running continued to provide relief from anxiety and escape from intrusive thoughts.

The only things I could not run from were the FBI and NYPD. They started showing up at the graduate dorm to whisk me back to NYC for more interrogation.

"Miss Scarpino, you are coming with us to NYC today," they'd say. "You are needed for more interrogations. Go pack your bags and come with us. You'll be gone for a few days. We have more questions for you and photographs to look at." That was it. I was supposed to stop my life and skip out on my responsibilities because they said so.

They never gave me advance notice, and I worried about what impression this was giving the administration at the graduate dorm. Valid worry. It was a bad impression. And that's how I lost my job as a residence counselor.

After I returned from one of these surprise trips to NYC, I was told by the administrators that my residence counselor position would end at the end of the semester and that I would have to find a place to live and funding if I wanted to continue in graduate school. My brother, Jon, and my graduate school advisor, who knew about the bombing, tried reasoning with them. Surely, they could not terminate my funding when I was a critical witness in a federal crime being investigated by the FBI.

"No," they said. "That wasn't the reason. She lost her position because she stole butter from the cafeteria. She does not set a good example to the other students in the dorm because she is a thief."

Perhaps I did take some butter, but everybody took butter, fruit, cookies, yogurt, and other small items we all paid for with our meal plan. It was so ridiculous and embarrassing, not to me but to Purdue University housing.

I thought they would understand the importance of my trips to New York and not penalize me for leaving the campus, especially when it was out of my control. But that's not how the people in the small town of Lafayette thought. Regardless of the reason, they didn't want a counselor involved with the FBI and NYPD. They would never admit to worrying that I was a felon or a fugitive, so they blamed it on the butter.

I now understand why I felt so overwhelmed and out of control. In a span of a few months, the naive, law-abiding Jane became a woman who was a suspect in a terrorist bombing, a fugitive, a flight risk, a major witness to a federal crime—and now a butter thief. I could not keep up with all these alter egos.

Who was I?

I had my faculty advisor and my brother in my corner. My advisor found me a position as a research assistant that paid for my tuition, and my brother, Jon, paid my rent for an off-campus apartment.

★   ★   ★

It took me two years to get my master's degree. I took a research option, meaning I had to do a research project, write a thesis, and defend it. I was in love with the idea of research and publishing, and Purdue was the place to embark on this endeavor. My hypervigilance served me well with my research. I became obsessed with it and was confident that my memory would not fail me in oral exams with material I had been engulfed in for two years. My graduate school committee knew about the bombing and my memory difficulties and had been very supportive.

In August 1979, I faced my graduate school committee to defend my research thesis on "Perception of Junctural Contrasts by Esophageal Speakers." I had been immersed in my research, so I was confident that I knew the material well and could fill any memory holes by referring to my data. That in itself was comforting. My oral exams went well, and I passed. There was one final question I had to answer from one of my professors, "Who is Jane Margaret Scarpino?"

This question made me realize that Christiane had become my identity. For the past two years, my professors called me Christi, the nickname I used for Christiane. Jane was gone. My professors questioned who Jane was, and I didn't know either. I expressed that it was my legal name. Honestly, I had no intention of calling myself Jane again because that person was lost. I was so shattered inside, trying to figure out who I was.

I was so proud of myself for coping with my flashbacks and memory problems to get my master's and publish my thesis. I'm not sure my parents were as proud or even aware of my struggles. Emotions were still not discussed in my family, as they assumed that any emotional problems made you weak. None of my family members made themselves available to me during my darkest time. I did not realize how disconnected that made me feel, but my mind was still in such chaos from the bombing that I didn't care. But my father made clear what he cared about and thought was important. My job choices. Money. Prestige.

I had several job offers in Indiana, but my father didn't like any of them. He never mentioned moving back East, but I preferred staying as far away from my father as possible. Distance between us made it easier to make my own decisions as long as I didn't give him details. I made the mistake of telling my father about my job offers in Gary, Indianapolis, and Fort Wayne.

"Don't take that job in Indianapolis," he said. "You won't make enough money, and you won't like the commute." Even though he knew absolutely nothing about salaries for a speech-language pathologist, he assumed I couldn't afford an apartment near my job. He believed it would be best if I stayed in my apartment in West Lafayette and commuted ninety minutes each way.

About a week later, I received a letter from my father with a check for $500.00 and an offer to buy me a car. I had gotten my driver's license, but my primary mode of transportation was my gray Columbia three-speed bicycle. Most people would have thought this was a loving gesture made by my father to help me get started. But I could see that it would pave the way for him to control my decisions. *I gave you money and a car; therefore, I have a say in everything you do.*

I ripped up the check, returned it, and declined his car offer. I was tired of people managing my life...my father, the FBI, the NYPD. I just wanted to make my own decisions and live my life without people butting in and telling me what I had to do and when to do it. I accepted a job at a state hospital in Fort Wayne, Indiana. I bought a car, found an apartment, and slept on the floor. I took a part-time job at Friendly's Restaurant so I could afford to buy a bed. I was happy making my own decisions. I gave my father my new address.

CHAPTER 6

THE STRUGGLE FOR CONTROL

M y transition to life in Fort Wayne was not as smooth as I had expected. On April 4, 1980, Marie Haydée Beltrán Torres (Sandra Peters) was arrested in Chicago with her husband and several other FALN members for involvement in bombings in NYC. She had been connected to the Mobil bombing based on her fingerprints on her employment application.

To this day, she is the only FALN member who has been positively linked with a bombing based on evidence. She was going to be tried for the bombing of the Mobil building and the murder of Charles Steinberg. The FBI needed me as a witness to prepare for her trial, so my time in Fort Wayne was constantly interrupted by FBI and NYPD agents showing up at my doorstep to take me back to NYC for questioning. I didn't comprehend just how important my role was in identifying Marie Torres until 2018 when I started researching the FALN for this book.

Even three years after the bombing, it was hard for me to believe I had confronted a terrorist and that the terrorist was a woman. I learned she was one month older than me and had a six-month-old baby. Even more disturbing was that she was living in Chicago, two hours away from me. I routinely flew into Chicago on my commutes between New York and Indiana. My assumption that I was at a safe distance from any terrorist was blown to bits—no pun intended.

How could I ever feel safe again?

I was fixated on the possibility of being caught in another terrorist attack. I wanted to be far from these violent people, but now I realized that they were never too far away. People have asked me if I was ever concerned about the FALN finding me and perhaps hurting me so that I couldn't provide any testimony against them. That thought never crossed my mind, and I am glad it did not. I was more worried about being killed in another bombing than ever worrying about FALN coming to get me.

I did not realize at the time that there would be an arising concern about other people coming to get me...the authorities.

One sunny afternoon in mid-April of 1980, I was home early since I had taken time off for a doctor's appointment. My phone was ringing, so I hurried to answer it.

"Hello?"

There was no voice on the other end, just breathing.

"Hello?"

Click. They hung up.

Must have been a wrong number.

Five minutes later, the phone rang again.

"Hello? Who is this?"

Click.

There was no caller I.D. with the landline. It was a mystery call.

About thirty minutes later, there was a heavy knock on my door. I could see the outline of a stocky, official-looking man through the glass in the door. "Miss Scarpino, I know you are home. Answer the door."

Oh crap...it's the sergeant I hate from the NYPD.

This was the man who always came to get me. He was a stocky man in his forties whose olive skin and sharp features made him look like he was of Italian descent. His loud, gruff voice was abrasive, and his arrogance rubbed me the wrong way. I couldn't stand him.

Now I knew who had called me and hung up. He wanted to be sure I was home because I was still considered a flight risk.

I opened the door. "Miss Scarpino, you need to come with me right now."

"I can't. I have to work tonight at the restaurant, and I have work tomorrow at my full-time job." I backed away and started to close the door separating us. "Every time I leave with you, I am docked pay. I won't be able to pay my rent this month."

The sergeant held on to the outside of the doorknob, preventing me from closing the door. His handcuffs made a clanging sound as they hit the door. "Miss Scarpino, there is an easy way and a hard way to do this. I hope you choose the easy way and come with me."

Based on past experiences and the sight of handcuffs, I knew what choice I had to make. I wanted to resist, but I knew that the handcuffs would win. I packed an overnight bag and went to NYC with the gruff sergeant I hated. There was no reason to threaten or intimidate me. I was an eighty-five-pound woman whom they needed to help convict a terrorist. I hadn't been considered a suspect for years, but I was still a critical witness. I was the one who took the real suspect's application with her fingerprints on it; I gave them the evidence they needed to connect her to the bombing.

Shouldn't they be handling me with kid gloves?

I flew to NYC with the sergeant, who took me to a hotel somewhere in Midtown Manhattan. He took me to my room, opened the door, and shut it behind me. The room was sparsely furnished with a bed, a chair, and a small desk. There was no telephone or TV. I did not find it comfortable with its bare walls and brown decor.

I sat around for a couple of hours, waiting for some sort of instructions or information about my visit and wondering when it would be time to eat. I opened the door to find a security officer standing outside my door.

"You can't leave," he said sternly, putting out his hand to stop me.

"Where can I get something to eat? Is there a place I can go for a quick snack?" My stomach had started to gurgle, which told me I needed to eat.

"You can't go anywhere," he said.

"Why? Can you bring me some food?" I put my hand on my stomach to try to squelch the noise.

"You can't go anywhere, and I can't get you anything," he said as he shifted his weight from one leg to the other.

I wondered if he was standing guard over me to protect or prevent me from leaving. He didn't say, and I didn't care. I wanted to quiet my now growling stomach.

"I'm starving. I need to eat." I opened my eyes as wide as I could to emphasize my point.

"I guess you can call for a pizza delivery," was his sarcastic reply.

I was now tired, hungry, and aggravated. "WHAT? How do I call when there is no phone in the room? Who is paying for this, the police department?"

He chuckled and told me I'd have to pay cash or use my credit card. I still had no idea how I'd place an order.

My hunger got the best of me, and I no longer wanted to be compliant and quiet. I needed to consider my own needs since nobody else was. Stand up for what you deserve— basic human rights. I mustered up my big girl voice.

"Wait just a minute. I assumed that since the NYPD brought me here and left me in this hotel, they would be feeding me, too."

I stiffened my spine in an effort to look taller and more assertive. "Nobody told me that I wasn't going to be able to go out. Nobody told me I was going to have to figure out where to get food and then pay for it myself."

The officer stood there with his arms folded and looked at me in disbelief. I threw my hands up in disgust.

I clasped my hands tightly behind my back. "I don't have any money with me. I don't own a credit card. So, I guess I'm not eating."

The officer stood there like a statue with a stupid grin.

I rolled my eyes and scoffed, "That means I'm not talking to anyone either. You can decide not to give me food or beverage, and I can decide I have nothing to say. I'm done."

I released my hands and pointed my right index finger at the officer.

"Tell your boss to fly me back to Indiana. You can't lock me in a room and not provide food or water. I'm done. Get me out of here," I said in a hostile tone.

I slammed the door, went over to the bed, and sat down.

Why is there always food deprivation involved with these guys? Here I am in an unidentified hotel, held against my will, and not given food or water. Why do I always get treated so poorly?

About an hour later, the man opened the door, carrying a brown paper bag containing a tuna salad sandwich and some chips. He gave me a Coke. Apparently, it was paid for. I was good for the night but had to repeat my performance a few more times to get food. Seriously. Even criminals get fed.

The next day, I found out that the reason I was brought to New York was to identify Marie Torres in a line-up and to prepare me to be a witness for her trial, which was scheduled for the following month of May. The criminal justice system needed me. Now that I knew this officially, I was sure I'd get some decent meals at the proper intervals, but NO! I waited for someone to say, "Can I get you something to eat, Miss Scarpino? Thank you for your time, Miss Scarpino. Can I get you anything?" I never heard those words. I had to continue to badger them for food. "I'm not talking until I eat" became my standard phrase. And then I'd be given some kind of a dry sandwich and Coke.

I wasn't nervous about identifying Marie Torres in a line-up. I had seen how it was done on TV, so I thought I could handle it.

I was brought into a small room with a one-way mirror. An officer explained that several women would be brought into the room behind the mirror. They explained that I would be able to see all of them, but they would not be able to see me.

I sat at the edge of my chair, ready to identify the woman who left her umbrella with the bomb in it at Mobil. Five or six women entered the room from the right to the left to form a line. Each one was handcuffed and accompanied by a man in uniform. Some were Hispanic, and some were White. They all had medium-length brown hair and were wearing pants and a shirt. These were my choices…a line of seemingly angry women squirming and pulling to get loose from the handcuffs. Viewing a line of uncooperative and combative women sent chills down my spine since it never occurred to me that women would act this way.

My skin felt like bugs were crawling all over it, and I started picking at it. The nausea and the pressure around my head were creeping back into my body.

My eyes went down the line, and I immediately spotted the woman I was looking for.

There she is. That one.

I held my breath as I pointed out Marie Haydée Beltrán Torres in the lineup. I recognized her without her wig and sunglasses. It was the look in her eyes. The same piercing look she had when we stood face to face in the Mobil office. Even though she couldn't see me, those dark brown eyes cut through me.

"Miss Scarpino, are you sure?" I was asked.

This time, that question empowered me instead of making me feel like a suspect or a victim. I wanted to point out the woman who left the bomb that killed Charles. I knew it was her. I had no doubts about what I saw. I pictured myself face-to-face with her in the Mobil office.

I felt sick to my stomach.

I just didn't understand how a woman my age could be a mother, a killer, and a terrorist. My head was spinning just thinking about it.

They never told me if my choice was correct, but I knew it was. My job was done, and I was sent home to Indiana with a US marshal. I was mentally and physically exhausted and still bothered about the whole food and money situation. My brain told me I should have felt angry, but I just felt defeated and numb.

That numbness seemed to have taken over my emotions. For decades after the bombing, I felt like I was pretending to live, playing the part of a "normal functioning" human being. I knew how I was supposed to feel and pretended to feel that way. It was all a big act that normalized my responses to the outside world. If I knew I was supposed to feel angry, I could act angry. This ability enabled me to function and gave me the confidence to self-advocate, but it never felt genuine or authentic. I had enough cognitive awareness of how one might respond in certain situations, so I attempted to perform those responses as needed. Now, I know that the emotional detachment I experienced is part of a response to trauma.

On the way home, I was drowning in my thoughts of feeling isolated and depressed. I was looking for something positive to happen that might snap me out of the doldrums and pop me back to my cheerful, positive self.

When I walked through my apartment door, I could see the blinking red light of my answering machine telling me that I had a message. I always checked the answering machine as soon as I got home. I loved the idea that some-one was leaving me a message when I was not there. Maybe this was the positive message I'd been waiting for! I pressed the button to check my messages; it was from my boss at Friendly's Restaurant.

"Hi Christi. We got a call from the New York Police Department about your recent trip to New York City. You've missed too many shifts, and we need someone reliable to close the restaurant. You've been replaced. We'll mail your last paycheck."

I was stunned. Now, I had lost the part-time job that I desperately needed. It's like the butter incident all over again. I already knew that my full-time job at the state hospital would dock my pay for the time in N.Y. I had only worked there a couple of months and had not earned any vacation or sick time yet. In fact, I was still a probation- ary employee, and I wondered if I would lose that job too. (Fortunately, I did not.)

The issue of not having enough money to pay my rent and buy food was now a crisis. I would lose my apartment if I didn't pay the rent, and my car would be repossessed if I failed to make payments on the loan. I dug out a business card from the NYPD and called the number. The phone rang a few times before I heard a man's voice answer the phone. "NYPD."

"Hello. This is Jane Scarpino. I am a witness for the Mobil Oil Bombing and would like to speak to the officer in charge of the investigation. I need to talk about my NYC trips and how I've been treated."

"Hold on, and I will have an officer speak with you."

My call was transferred to an officer higher up in the chain of command.

"What can I do for you, Miss Scarpino?"

And then I let loose.

"First of all, don't ever send that sergeant to pick me up again. He made prank phone calls and then showed up at my door with HANDCUFFS, threatening me about an easy way and a hard way to go with him. That is crazy!"

I took a deep breath, and more angry-sounding words came out. "Why can't I be notified in advance, be given time to pack, and be given time to notify my employers?"

I paused for a second, cleared my throat, and filled my lungs with air to continue my rant.

"AND because of you, I have lost my part-time job at Friendly's Restaurant. I also lose a day of pay from my regular job every time I have to go to N.Y. That amount is adding up! I have lost so much money because of you, and I can't afford to pay my rent and car loan this month." My voice started to quiver as my speech became louder and more rapid.

"Then, when I get to New York, I'm told I can't go any-where, call anyone, or leave to get food. I'm told I can have food delivered, but I have to pay for it myself. EXCUSE ME??? Where do you think the money is coming from? A day of eating out in New York costs more than a week's worth of groceries for me."

Silence on the other end of the phone. I take another deep breath and finish.

"I haven't been compensated for anything, and I should be. I should not have to pay for anything. I also need to be compensated for my time. This has all happened to me because YOU need me to help you. Loss of a job. Loss of income. Loss of respect from my employers. They think I'm some sort of criminal. I'm done with you people."

Silence.

More silence.

Finally, the officer grunted out a reply. "We sent that sergeant to pick you up because we thought you liked him. He told us he had a good relationship with you. We can't notify you in advance because you are a flight risk. We need you to stay in the U.S."

"Like him? Oh my god. I hate that sergeant. He tries to intimidate me, telling me there's an easy way and a hard way to leave with him and flashing a set of handcuffs at me. We have no relationship. He's a mean, gruff man. I never want to see him again. And I'm not going anywhere. My father sent me to Bermuda for a vacation after the bombing. I had no idea that would make me a flight risk forever. I'm telling you, I'm not going anywhere. Quit the surprise visits. I've lost a job and may lose my full-time job because of you."

"Would you feel better if we sent US marshals from Indianapolis to pick you up? We don't have to send the sergeant."

"Yes, I could deal with that, but only if I am notified ahead of time…maybe a day in advance so that I could be ready. No threats of handcuffs."

"We can arrange that."

I still was not satisfied. I was not done with my rant.

"One more thing—the money. I can't afford to buy my own food in New York City, plus you make it impossible for me to access food, even if I could get it myself. I can't make ends meet because of all the pay I have lost and will continue to lose. What am I supposed to do?"

Silence again. I waited for him to say, "Are you sure this is what happened, Miss Scarpino?" but he did not. He put me on hold.

When he returned to the call, he said, "You will be provided with three meals per day that will be paid for.

Send me a list of your lost wages. You will be back-compensated, and we'll reimburse you for your lost pay from now on. Is that acceptable?"

"Yes," I replied as I patted myself on the back for successfully advocating for myself.

I really wanted to say NO just to be defiant, but he gave in to my demands. On future trips, I did get reimbursed for lost wages and was fed. The US marshals who picked me up for these trips called me in advance and were very pleasant.

Once again, I realized how much power my words could have. It just took an awful lot out of me to finally get the words out. Although I knew my words were powerful, I questioned whether I was worthy of speaking. It used to be so easy to express my thoughts and feelings. That had changed. It took effort now. *Everything* took so much effort.

Despite acting assertively with the NYPD, I felt I was losing control. I could make myself appear calm and assertive in public, but I was acting. Talking about the bombing had become so painful that I felt like my insides were ripping apart. I knew that I would have to describe the bombing at least one more time next month at the federal trial for Marie Torres. I was not sure how I was going to get through it.

CHAPTER 7

IT SHOULD BE OVER NOW

On May 18, 1980, the US marshals from Indianapolis picked me up in Fort Wayne to take me to New York City. I had advance notice of this trip, so I was packed and ready to go. I hoped this was my last trip, but I knew it would likely be the most difficult yet. I was going to testify in the federal trial of Marie Haydée Beltrán Torres, which meant I would see her again in person—this time, no disguises and no one-way mirrors.

As I was headed to NYC on the plane, my head overflowed with questions about the approaching experience.

How would I feel when I saw her?

What would she do or say when she heard my testimony?

Would she remember me?

Will I be able to tell my story in front of so many people?

Then the fear set in...

What if I start to relive the bombing?

How will I get through this alone?

I knew I would be sequestered, so I would not be able to be with or talk to anyone. No one would be there for me. I'd have to manage my emotions and flashbacks by myself. I was not sure I could do this. I was not going to be able to use running or my work as strategies to alleviate my anxiety. Those were my primary ways of getting through the day. Perhaps I could tap into strategies I learned from my prior therapist in college, Janet.

I sat back in my seat, plugged in the headphones, and listened to classical music. *These are just thoughts*, I told myself. *You can control your thoughts. Put these thoughts in a box and shut the lid tightly. Put the box in the closet and focus on the music.*

I found myself breathing in and breathing out slowly and imagining myself on that sunny, warm beach as Janet had taught me. *I will use the imagery of the beach and rolling waves to get through this.*

Once I landed in New York, I was met at the airport by US marshals and taken to a hotel somewhere in the city to be sequestered. This was all too familiar, except the NYPD sergeant I disliked was absent. Once again, I was in a sparse hotel room with only a bed, chair, and desk. There was no phone or television. I could not call anyone or see anyone. I could not leave the room, and someone was standing guard outside my door.

I had no understanding of the rationale for my isolation. At that time, had I understood that I was sequestered because I was a key witness in a federal investigation of a terrorist, my perspective might have been different. I would have felt empowered because I was making an important contribution to the federal trial. Instead, the lack of explanation left me feeling downtrodden. I felt like I was on trial, although I was not. My mental health was suffering—and the lack of information provided to me didn't help.

A chicken salad sandwich was brought to my hotel room for dinner, and I tried to settle in for a good night's sleep in preparation for the trial scheduled for the following day. As I climbed into the hard hotel bed, all those thoughts I put in the imaginary box in the closet came rushing into my head. I could feel the sweat oozing through my pores and dripping onto the bed sheets.

I forced myself to imagine that Janet was with me and helping me through the steps of Progressive Relaxation. I initiated a sequence of deep inhalations/exhalations while tensing and relaxing my muscles.

Take deep breaths to the count of three.

In	*one*	*two*	*three*
Out	*one*	*two*	*three*
In	*one*	*two*	*three*
Out	*one*	*two*	*three*
In	*one*	*two*	*three*
Out	*one*	*two*	*three*

By the end of the third breath cycle, the sensation of something building up in my throat made me leap out of bed. I grabbed my throat with both hands in an effort to stop the intense gagging that surfaced. Running to the bathroom, I tasted chicken and mayonnaise on its way up my esophagus and out of my mouth. How ironic...when I finally get food without demanding, I vomit. I rinsed out my mouth and, although I was feeling dizzy and hot, made my way back to the hard bed with the flat pillow. I fell asleep with the palm of my hand covering my necklace.

✳   ✳   ✳

The next thing I knew, daylight was filtering through the dirty window.

May 19, 1980, was the first day of a four-day federal trial. I had never been in a courtroom before and had little understanding of the judicial process other than what I had seen on TV and a couple of times when I appeared (but was not selected) for jury duty. This was nothing like Perry Mason. I was not prepared emotionally for what was about to happen.

My memory did not absorb all the details of the four days of court proceedings. But there were a few scenes that are ingrained in my memory forever.

When I was seated in the courtroom on the first day, I was surprised to see that it was filled with people, many of whom I would soon learn were her followers and support-ers of her cause to free Puerto Rico. They considered her a prisoner of war and were there to support her.

I had thought my testimony would only be heard by the judge, the jury, and the defendant, Marie Torres. I expected to see Marie Torres sitting quietly, acting nervous and per-haps quietly fumbling with her hands as she did when I saw her in the Mobil office. Instead, I saw the petite Marie Torres standing up and yelling vehemently in Spanish while wildly waving her arms. I could feel her anger; she was clearly in warrior mode for her cause and to rally support from her followers in the courtroom.

Her behavior continued to escalate, somewhat like a tantrum exhibited by a two-year-old. I had never seen an adult carry on like this before. After she did not respond to the judge's repeated commands to sit down, she was surrounded by US marshals. While she was standing and yelling, they picked her up and moved her to another room where she would listen to the court proceedings through a speaker. Suddenly, the room was silent; everyone was seated, and I realized I would not have to look at her when I was speaking. I was so relieved.

Years after the trial, I learned that Marie Torres was yell-ing that she would not participate in the trial because she thought it violated her Constitutional rights. She claimed to be a prisoner of war and, thus, refused the right to an attor-ney and to participate in the trial. I cannot comprehend the rationale behind her thinking other than it was the aberrant thinking of a terrorist. Terrorists do not accept individual responsibility for their actions. They are brainwashed into thinking that their cause justifies their actions, even if they personally caused destruction and death. They never feel personally responsible, have no remorse, and never believe that legal consequences are justified. There is no negotiation with terrorists. They don't care about the consequences. They only care that they have made their political point of view known, even if that includes violence and death. They are willing to kill and be killed for their cause. Death has little meaning to them.

I don't remember how many of the four days I was actually present for the trial. I can verify that I took the witness stand at least twice because of court drawings of me wearing two different outfits on the stand. I remember the times I was on the stand, but otherwise, my memory is blank. The experience itself was so emotionally overwhelming and triggering that unless I was being spoken to directly (as in questioning and cross-examination), I blocked out the rest.

Of the times I was on the stand, I do remember, quite vividly, sitting on a hard bench behind a podium to the judge's left. Over to my left was a large, standing easel with a flip chart. I was looking directly at a diagram of the employment office at Mobil Oil. The prosecutor, a distinguished-looking man in a dark suit, stood before me.

"Miss Scarpino, please tell the court what happened on the day of August 3, 1977." He pointed to the diagram. "Please explain the diagram you see and use it in your description."

I described the office layout as it was pictured on the diagram. I described my encounter with Marie Torres, my interaction with Charles and Ivan, and then the explosion. It became more and more vivid as I spoke...

The diagram disappeared in my mind, and I was no longer in the courtroom...

I'm lying next to the philodendron.

How did I get here?

I can see its large, green leaves above me, surrounded by smoke and thick, gray haze.

The smell of gunpowder is sickening.

There is blood everywhere.

There are pieces of furniture and ceiling tiles all around me.

I'm not sure what brought me back to the moment exactly, but somehow, my testimony was over. And somewhere along the way, I had begun to cry.

"Thank you, Miss Scarpino. That's all for now."

I continued to cry uncontrollably as I was escorted from the witness box. My fingers navigated to the ruby and diamond on my necklace, which reminded me that I was alive and safe.

✶   ✶   ✶

After the trial was over, the US marshals took me to the airport in New York and put me on a flight back to Indianapolis, where more US marshals met me and drove me back to my apartment in Fort Wayne.

I returned to work the next day at the state hospital like nothing had happened. Nobody, not even my family, asked me about my trip or how I felt. Maybe they were told not to. Perhaps they were afraid to ask. I didn't want to talk about it anyway, at least not with friends and coworkers.

On May 22, 1980, Marie Torres was convicted of placing the bomb in the Mobil building that killed Charles Steinberg and injured several others. She was charged with seditious conspiracy or attempting to overthrow the US government and sentenced to life in prison. (In 1997, she filed an appeal to vacate her sentence because she was denied her Constitutional rights under the Fifth, Sixth, and Eighth Amendments. Her appeal was denied, but she was released from prison on parole in 2009.)

Eventually, most of the people involved with the bombing were arrested, found guilty of seditious conspiracy, and incarcerated. And then, in 1999, sixteen were pardoned and released by President Clinton in exchange for promising they wouldn't engage in terrorism. The leader of FALN, Oscar López Rivera, was then pardoned and released by President Obama on January 17, 2017. FALN members have not been openly active with additional bombings since, but for all any of us know, they could be involved in underground activity.

In 1980, I was glad that the trial was over, but I did not realize that the flashbacks and anxiety would persist for many years. I honestly thought that since my life would no longer be disrupted by trips to NYC and interactions with the FBI and NYPD, my flashbacks would go away. I thought that Marie Torres's life sentence would close the door to the trauma I had experienced.

I knew the trauma was living inside of me, and I couldn't just dismiss it. And now, here I was, after the completion of the trial, thinking that now that it was over,

I would be all better. Maybe I thought because "justice was served," the trauma chapter of my life was complete, and I could move on.

I rejected people's comments that I should be "over it" since I survived and the bombing was over. I rejected people's advice to "forgive and forget." I don't think I can ever forgive Marie Torres. Other people's remarks made me question my strength and resilience, but now I can see that I should have never doubted myself. I was not the weak person others were making me out to be. I could withstand the pressure of being a lead witness in a federal trial while completing a master's degree, publishing a thesis, starting a career, and living independently. I had coped with the effects of a mental illness that I had to silently endure without much support and validation. That required tenacity, determination, and fortitude. I was a powerful young woman with a strong spirit.

Now that I felt the ordeal of the trial was over, I wanted to move on with my life, but I felt stuck. Making decisions was hard. Getting out of bed in the morning was hard. Going to sleep at night was hard. I felt out of place in Indiana. Maybe the reality was that I just felt out of place...period. I was still looking for myself. Maybe I needed to return to a more familiar place where I thought I would be more comfortable. I decided I needed to move back East. It was time to look for a new job.

CHAPTER 8

TIME FOR A CHANGE

In the summer of 1980, I found the perfect job at Burbank Hospital in Fitchburg, Massachusetts. Luck had it that I went to graduate school with my new boss, which put me at ease. She knew me well, and we had a good relationship while we were at Purdue.

My days in Massachusetts were filled with routines that enabled me to focus on my daily activities. I'd wake up every morning with the same thought: *I am a survivor of a terrorist attack. I don't feel good. I don't want to get out of bed.* Next, I would wonder what triggers would present themselves and send me into a panic attack or, even worse, cause me to dissociate. I'd try to plan strategies to avoid triggers to keep me on an even keel; however, sometimes, triggers appeared out of nowhere, and strategies were not effective.

One morning, as I lay in bed, I stretched my arms over my head and glanced at my alarm clock. It was 6:30 a.m.

That gave me an hour to get ready before leaving for work at 7:30. I wanted to stay in bed longer, but I knew I had to get to work. Yawning, I held onto the teardrop necklace as a reminder that I was still in the present. I tapped my forehead to see if I could stop the persistent buzzing noise reverberating between my ears, which seemed to be a residual from my past. I hated that the past was intruding into my present and I couldn't dismiss it. I felt like something was eating at my brain and my heart, which rendered me helpless. I made myself get out of bed and walked into the bathroom. As I brushed my teeth, I reviewed all the sticky notes I had placed on the bathroom mirror.

"Celebrate the positive."

"Love yourself."

"You are worth it."

"Old ways won't open new doors."

"When the past comes knocking at your door, don't answer it."

"You are smart."

"You can do anything."

Starting my day with positive self-talk helped get me moving. I got dressed and went to the kitchen for breakfast. Sitting at the small table and sipping my black coffee, I read through my daily to-do lists. I had become the keeper of copious lists and considered myself the queen of organization to compensate for my memory. I never remembered what I did the previous day or what I had to do that day, so the result was keeping an ongoing list of tasks and multiple calendars for work-related and personal appointments.

My need to have several ongoing to-do lists was a compulsive behavior that took up two or more hours per day of my time. I'd review my lists every hour, hoping I could check something off as being done. I usually added more tasks than I checked off because I would then have more to keep me busy.

When I was satisfied that I had a plan for the day, I got into my car to drive to work.

I turned the key in the ignition and started driving. The car radio was on, and I wasn't paying attention until I heard the words *violent attack*. In all of a second, my body was engulfed with that squeezing pressure, my eyes were tearing, and my eardrums felt ready to explode. I gasped for air. I couldn't breathe.

I pulled over and sat there in my car. I opened the driver's side door and threw up on the ground. I realized that I had just experienced an anxiety attack. My fingers located the ruby teardrop in my necklace, and I knew I was OK. I just needed a few minutes to compose myself.

Closing the car door and wiping off my face with an old tissue, I finished my drive to work. I punched in on time and then spent my day working with people with communication problems. Working with other people and their problems took that focus away from myself, and that made me happy—especially today when I experienced a panic attack.

Work ended at a quarter to five, and I drove back to my apartment. Back home, my work thoughts had now been replaced with that persistent buzzing noise that I woke up with. It was like a loud tinnitus in my brain instead of my ears.

Keeping busy distracted me from the noise, so I always planned several things to do once I arrived home after work.

Arriving home, I checked my evening to-do list. First on the list was "eat." I opened the fridge and heated some macaroni and cheese in the microwave. Good enough.

Next on the list—"go running." After I changed into my shorts and top, I slipped on my blue Adidas and bolted out the door. I planned to run the ten-mile stint to the Twin City Plaza. That took me about eighty minutes, and then I could check it off my list.

After getting home from my run, I continued going through the list, checking off each item as completed. *Shower, summarize my day in my journal, revise my to-do lists for the next day, and find additional positive affirmations to post on my mirror.* On this particular night, I spent more time with my journal, writing about the impact my panic attack had on my day. Starting my day with a panic attack made me feel anxious for the rest of my day and worried that I would encounter another trigger. I always tried to avoid the radio and TV because I was aware that news of violence could set off a panic attack or flashback. I felt guilty and punished myself emotionally for failing to protect myself by turning off the car radio. I hadn't yet accepted that triggers could pop up at any time, and I might not be able to avoid them.

The next day would start the same and end the same. This is how my days went for the next decade.

I worked hard at keeping my flashbacks, memory problems, and anxiety a secret. I felt like I was two people: the responsible person who held down a good job and appeared to be "on top of the world" and the emotionally fragile person who was mentally hanging by a thread. I needed to keep that delicate part of me concealed because I was worried that someone would find out and I might lose everything I valued, such as my job, my apartment, and my friends.

As I've mentioned earlier, in the 1970s and 1980s, there was a lot of stigma attached to mental illness. People with mental illness were often thought of as crazy or even dangerous. The focus of care for people with mental illness was in institutional settings. While living in Fort Wayne, I worked in one such institution, a state hospital with over 900 residents. At the time, I thought some of the people I worked with could have lived in the community with supports. However, there was very little in the way of supports and services in the community for people with mental illness. I certainly did not want to end up in an institution. Institutions at that time were not therapeutic and were detrimental to social development and rehabilitation. Once you were admitted, there was little to no chance of getting out. I knew this was not the right avenue for me, so I had to hide my difficulties so no one would find out and suggest that I be admitted. Society did not tolerate people with mental health problems, so I felt forced to conceal my true self.

Running and my work were the two things I looked forward to every day. I made so many friends through both. My running friends encouraged me to run even more, which just fell right into my hypervigilant tendencies. I had become somewhat of a celebrity in the running world, and several newspaper articles were written about my ultramarathon runs (racing distances beyond 26.2 miles).

An article in the *Worcester Telegram* described me as putting more mileage on my running shoes than on my car. In October of 1981, *The Montachusett Review* described me as "The Little Giant" because, at four feet and eleven inches, I had achieved "giant feats" by completing fifty-mile road races. Most female runners at the time were tall and muscular. I was short and petite. In 1981, *Ultra Running Magazine* ranked me twenty-fourth in North America in the annual standings for running fifty miles (eight hours and two minutes) and twentieth in the fifty-kilometer standings for women. I also held the records for running fifty miles and fifty kilometers for the Central Massachusetts Striders Running Club.

I never would have run that much if I had not been using the sport to cope. The endorphins from long-distance running made me feel powerful and great. It was a time when I could just pay attention to the rhythms of my breathing and my body moving. I didn't think about anything. It was a moving meditation for me. The recognition I received for being a great runner made me feel normal—because running didn't include my struggles with memory or coping with flashbacks.

Although running got me through many days, I did pursue structured cognitive therapy because of my many sleepless nights, flashbacks, and never feeling safe. I would not read the newspaper or watch television because any suggestion of violence would send me into a flashback.

The word *flashback* wasn't even that accurate because I wasn't *thinking* about the Mobil bombing. I *re-lived* the Mobil bombing and felt like I was there.

I was hoping that cognitive therapy could help me get rid of those flashbacks and the other things that I did (or didn't do) that affected my life, such as not going to movies, avoiding crowds, and staring at the wrinkled two-by-two-inch newspaper photo of Marie Torres that I carried in my wallet. Every time I looked at her picture, I felt weak and nauseous, yet I was compelled to look at her several times per day. It was a repetitive behavior (like checking my to-do lists every day) that helped me cope with anxiety. Now, I can see that I exhibited behaviors associated with obsessive-compulsive disorder (OCD), which often occurs in people with a history of trauma.

I knew these were not normal behaviors, but I couldn't stop doing them. Now, I can clearly see that I was overcome with intrusive thoughts and images related to the bombing, which made me very anxious. I tried to ignore my fixation on Marie Torres's photo and modify my behaviors, but I could not. I needed to find a therapist who could help me.

After trying different therapists, I finally connected with Dr. Claudia Siebel, whom I saw for almost thirty years. She asked me hard questions, and most of the time, I had no answers. Her questions and comments made me uncomfortable, but they also made me think.

Questions like...Why *did* I carry a photo of Marie Torres in my wallet? Why did I avoid TV and radio when I could select my channels or turn them off? Why did I avoid magazines when I could choose the content or just close the magazine? I realized that some of my fears and avoidance behaviors were irrational. I realized that looking at Marie Torres's mug shot every time I opened my wallet was not helpful. I discovered my behavior was unreasonable, but I couldn't stop it.

I used to have incredible self-control and could modify my actions and behavior if I wanted to. I was not capable of doing that anymore as a result of my trauma. I did things and had rituals that I couldn't explain. Those behaviors didn't benefit me, but I couldn't stop doing them. If someone had explained to me that I had OCD tendencies and PTSD, it would have made more sense to me. I might have been able to cope better knowing that there was a reason for my behavior. But my behaviors were never explained to me. I just thought I was crazy.

It bothered me that I had to look at the photo of Marie Torres several times per day. I tried not to look at it and even made deals with myself to stop looking. Even with therapy, this behavior seemed to be a losing battle. Dr. Siebel and I discussed my preoccupation with the photo many times because my thoughts about looking at her photo were so intrusive that I could not think about anything else. I'd finally give in, open my wallet, look at the tiny black-and-white photo, and feel a sense of relief and control.

And then, one day, I conquered this photo-looking ritual. I was finally able to integrate our discussions in therapy with my behavior.

I'm ready to stop this.

I opened my wallet and pulled out the tiny, crumpled photo of Marie Torres. I quickly glanced at it, ripped it into small pieces, and threw it in the trash. I let out a big sigh as I felt like the weight of the world was lifted from my shoulders.

I finally am separated from the person who has ruined my life.

In 1981, I started dating John, an engineer for the telephone company. He called me Christi, even though he knew my real name was Jane. I told him about my past, and it didn't seem to matter to him. After two years, we became engaged and planned our wedding for September 1984.

In my efforts for self-care, I spent time thinking about what my soul needed, my beliefs about the world/universe, and who I was. My name was deeply entwined into all of this. Anyone's name is a big part of their identity. Your name represents everything about YOU. When people say your name, you have thoughts and feelings about who you are.

Jane had not been my real identity since August 3, 1977. I knew Jane was no longer who I was when I talked to my mom about changing my name. Now, it was 1984. I still didn't know who the old person (Jane) was, and I wasn't sure who the new person, Christi, was. What I did know was that I legally wanted to change my name to match what most people knew me as, which was Christi.

In May of 1984, I started the legal process to change my name to Christiane. The day the letter of approval came from the probate court, I was so relieved. I no longer had to tell people to call me Christi or Christiane or explain why I didn't want to be called Jane.

There it was in writing. Jane Margaret Scarpino was legally changed to Christiane Jane Scarpino. My name change made me feel like I was finally one person. I left Jane behind. I was officially Christiane.

I felt like I was closer to my real identity with the name change, but there were social implications that I wasn't prepared for. Most people who knew me before the bombing still called me Jane. I tried to explain how I no longer identified with that person, but they would respond with, "You'll always be Jane to me." People did not understand or couldn't accept that I had changed. People who met me after 1977 knew me as Christi or Christiane, which was how I introduced myself.

I also did not realize the impact my name change would have on legal documents such as my driver's license, social security card, and marriage license. I had planned a wedding for the fall, and now, my legal first name was different. Changing it on the marriage license was easy. Convincing the minister to call me Christiane in the ceremony was not so easy. When we had completed the paperwork to be married by this minister, I had to use my legal name, which, at the time, was Jane. I also had to supply my birth and baptismal certificates, which listed Jane Margaret as my first and middle names. My fiancé, John, and I made an appointment with the minister of the church we attended to discuss my name change.

John and I walked into the minister's chambers to present our request.

We sat down in the cushioned chairs across from the minister, and I said, "I was in the process of changing my first name legally, and the change came through now. So please call me Christiane during the ceremony instead of Jane."

"Weren't you baptized as Jane Margaret?" he said, looking over his black glasses.

"Well, yes, I was, but my first name is legally changed. And it has been approved as a legal name change by the court."

As he looked over the top of his black glasses, he insisted, "I shall call you by your baptized name during the ceremony as that is your God-given name."

I shifted in my chair and crossed my legs, so I was sitting on one hip. "Well, that is not who I am anymore. If you insist on calling me Jane during the ceremony, we will have to find someone else to preside over the wedding." That was a risky statement because it would mean finding another person to officiate the ceremony in that church or finding a different venue altogether in less than a month.

"Well," he sighed and swiveled in his chair to face John, "What do you think of all of this name-changing?"

In his calm manner, John said, "I am fine with this. I am marrying Christi, and I'm happy to have her called Christiane during the ceremony because that is who I am marrying."

I was quite taken aback that the minister sought my fiancé's approval. The sour thought popped into my head.... *If I have the legal right to change my first name, why do I need a man's permission to use it? How can a religion and a man decide what name I shall be called?* Honestly, this type of thinking was the driving force that eventually changed me into an agnostic.

The minister expelled a huge sigh. "Well, since you agree, I will use Christiane during the ceremony if I can somewhere mention that she was formerly known as Jane Margaret. Let's look at the ceremony and see where we can say that."

For the sake of the wedding, I did not argue the point, swallowed my pride, and agreed to use both names. That problem was solved, but an issue remained—my father. I had not yet told him that I legally changed my name, and I was worried that he would not approve and might even refuse to come. Even though he did come to the wedding and was pleasant, he called me Jane Margaret for as long as he lived.

I never took my husband John's last name because I thought that changing my first and last names would be too hard, and he didn't care. I also wasn't ready to give up Scarpino. That was one part of my name that had been constant and that I had identified with. John and I had talked about the bombing, and he accepted the reasons for my name change, accepted my going to therapy, and accepted my quirks.

★   ★   ★

At age twenty-nine, many of my friends were getting married. I felt like it was time to settle down, and getting married seemed like the right thing to do at my age. So, when John asked me to marry him, I said "yes," and I married a man who looked good on paper. All the boxes were checked, all the *i*'s were dotted, and all the *t*'s were crossed. We got married, bought a house together with a yard, and bought a dog—a Boston Terrier. (Little did I know this dog would ignite my passion for dogs.) But there was an important piece missing: emotions.

Although I thought I was in love and said I was in love, I didn't feel it. I realize that now, but I didn't know that then. John was perfect on paper, so I should have been in love with him, or so I thought. My decision to marry John was not based on emotion but on logic and reasoning.

Around the time we wed, I was no longer leaving as many sticky notes with positive affirmations all over the house, but I still was very rigid with scheduling and wanting things to be "in order." I still made copious to-do lists on a daily basis. In that regard, John and I were similar. He was an engineer who liked routines and consistency and was also a list-maker. We seemed perfect for one another. We both had professional careers and the same philosophy about money management, and we were raised in the Methodist religion. Our separate families and friends liked each other.

Our marriage lasted for four years. My difficulty perceiving emotions made it difficult for me to recognize our communication breakdowns and the fact that we were drifting apart. After two years, I realized our relationship was in trouble, but I couldn't figure out how to "fix" us. I suggested that we go to marital counseling, and John refused. I was still getting therapy for myself, and John thought I was the only one who needed the treatment. I tried to explain that marital counseling would be for the both of us to work on our relationship together. He didn't want to talk about it. He obviously didn't understand that it was up to both of us to work on our marital problems. He blamed me for our lack of communication and interaction but was unwilling to discuss it. We couldn't communicate, so we went our separate ways in 1988.

✹   ✹   ✹

After my divorce was final, I needed a break, and the perfect opportunity arose for a trip. My brother, Jon, was getting married in Hawaii that same year, so I planned a three-week trip, which included a cruise around the Hawaiian islands, time in Honolulu for the wedding preparations, and then a trip to Maui. I expected there to be family drama that would be stressful for me, and I needed to plan time to decompress. My brother was marrying a woman almost thirty years younger. My parents were attending the wedding, and my father did not approve. My mother told me that he didn't approve of my divorce either. So, tension was high.

I was so excited about the cruise. This was my first cruise, and I couldn't wait for the sea and salt air to clear my mind and help me relax.

I flew to Oahu and boarded the U.S.S. Constitution, a small cruise ship that docked on the islands of Oahu, Maui, Kauai, and Hawaii. To my surprise, there were lots of activities for singles, which I attended just to have fun. I had no interest in starting any romance.

When we docked in Kauai on the second morning, one of the officers took me aside and whispered in my ear, "After dinner tonight, we are having a Meet the Officers party. I think you will like one of our engineers. His name is Mouse. He's from New Jersey."

I spent the day biking around Kauai, picnicking, and snorkeling; then, I returned to the ship to prepare for dinner and to meet Mouse. *Why do they call him Mouse? Is he quiet as a mouse? Is he small? Does he like cheese?*

My questions were answered after dinner when I was introduced to Mouse. His name was Bill Maus, and Mouse was his nickname. He had sandy blonde hair, and I thought he looked pretty handsome in his white, pressed uniform. As one of the ship's engineers, he offered to give me a tour of the vessel, including the engine room and the bridge. Afterward, we danced all night in the disco on the ship. We saw each other every night for the rest of the week. I wasn't even thinking of a ship romance, but it happened.

After the week was over, Bill asked for my address and phone number and promised to call me. I obliged, hoping he would call but not thinking he would. I had read about these ship romances. The officers and crew would date a new person on every cruise. Bill said this wasn't the case, but why would it be different? Relaxed and renewed, I left the idea of Bill behind and continued on to Honolulu for Jon and Janet's wedding.

The wedding was lovely, and there was surprisingly no family conflict. My father's response to my divorce from John was kind and accepting, which was confusing to me as I expected judgment and a lecture. Maybe that was how he wanted me to remember him; he died of a heart attack on the front lawn at his home in Maine in October 1989.

This came as a shock to the family. We knew that my father had a heart condition, but he made light of it. His funeral was one of the last times that all four of us siblings were together with my mother. Nobody said much. Nobody cried. He was a difficult man to live with, and I think all of us, including my mother, experienced a sense of relief.

My father was buried in the cemetery in Thomaston, Maine. After the graveside service, we returned to their house, approximately fifteen miles away in Port Clyde. We asked my mother if she needed our help with anything, and she responded that we could start moving the furniture she hated into the garage. My mom clearly asserted her identity by decorating the house to her liking. From that day forward, she lived in the rambling, five-bedroom house overlooking the ocean by herself, and she thrived.

CHAPTER 9

TERROR IN THE SHADOWS

B ill Maus never called, but ten years later, in 1998, I found myself married a second time. Life was much the same in the ten years between the cruise and my second marriage. I still started my days with positive affirmations (although not on sticky notes), kept multiple to-do lists and schedules, and planned my day to the second.

The main difference was that running had become less of a focus, and showing dogs had become my passion. I established my love for dogs and a new hobby of breeding and showing Boston Terriers. I owned a big house with five acres of land in Ashburnham, Massachusetts, where I had established a show kennel with anywhere from seven to twenty Boston Terriers there at one time. I never dreamed that this hobby would be the primary focus of my life and would eventually replace running as a coping mechanism. My love of dogs led me to breed fifty-six litters, finish twenty champions, and get several performance titles on my dogs.

I became an American Kennel Club (AKC) judge for confor-
mation and Junior Showmanship and a hunting-retriever
judge for the United Kennel Club. When you are this
involved with dogs, it becomes a lifestyle.

I identified as a dog person; most of my friends were in
the dog show/breeding community. The thread that held us
together was our common interest in dogs. That was the main
focus of conversation and the reason for our interactions. No
one knew me as a survivor of a terrorist attack, and I didn't
have to pretend to be "normal" or mask my emotional states.
"Normal" in the dog community is living your life around
your dogs. In that respect, I was the same as everybody else,
which normalized me. It was a very comfortable, emotional
place for me.

I spent a lot of time on the road showing dogs with my
good friend and professional handler, Phyllis. I started dating her son, who was a few years younger than me, and after
about a year, we became engaged. All my friends in the dog
community thought we were the perfect match. He grew up
with multiple dogs, as his mother, Phyllis, owned a boarding
kennel, bred Beagles, and was a professional handler. He
certainly understood what it was like to have multiple dogs
and be a part of the show world. More boxes checked off.
My best friend would be my mother-in-law. My soon-to-be
husband loved dogs and didn't mind living with twenty of
them. He started helping me in the show ring. The outside
world approved of our relationship, and I didn't want to be
alone. I thought this second marriage was a great idea.

*   *   *

At this time, in addition to my hobby of training and show-ing dogs, I was working in a small private school for chil-dren with multiple disabilities. One morning, the school received a telephone call that there was a bomb threat in the building. Staff immediately started the building evacuation, which consisted of moving two floors of children in wheel-chairs out of the building. I moved swiftly with the other staff to get the children out of the building, never thinking twice about what I needed to do for the children. Thoughts of my own past experience were set aside as I pushed wheel-chairs out of the building and into the parking lot. And this is where I started to have a hard time.

We were told to move the students about forty feet from the front door. Knowing what a bomb can do, I ques-tioned the proximity of the people to the building. This is the same place we went for fire drills, but this was not a fire drill. I questioned our location with the school principal and was told we were fine. I took out the keys to my car and fingered my necklace. I knew I shouldn't leave, but I didn't want to stay either. It took all the strength that I had to stand out there with the children. I needed to stay with them because it was my job to keep them safe. The princi-pal went back into the building and disappeared for about fifteen minutes.

When she came back outside, she declared that the building was safe and that we should return to class.

Wait a minute, I thought. *The police and the fire depart-ment were not called. This principal thinks she has the ability to detect a bomb when a highly trained NYPD Bomb Squad managed to miss it altogether?*

My heart started racing as I clutched my necklace for the second time. *This thirty-something principal is willing to accept responsibility for the lives of one hundred physically disabled students. She is not taking the bomb threat seriously.*

I felt I needed to say something. As I walked towards her, my breaths became short and shallow, insufficient to fill my lungs. When I was about two feet away from her, I felt like I was going to choke.

She made eye contact with me, and with her usual big grin, she said, "What's up, Christi? You don't look so good."

Nodding my head in agreement, all I could manage to force out was, "I'm going home." I wished I could say more, but I was struggling to breathe.

"That's fine, but you will have to take a full sick day since it is before noon," she informed me.

I said no more. I quickly turned around and ran to my car, keys still in hand. I jumped into the driver's seat.

Several minutes later, I found myself at home and in bed, fully clothed. My new husband had gone away for the week, so I was home alone. I stayed in bed until late that night, when I finally ate a donut, drank some water, and took a shower. I felt the need to write down a positive affirmation on a sticky note: "Do what is right for you." I placed it on the bathroom mirror.

The next day, I returned to a normal workday. Before classes started, I went into the principal's office and said, "I want to explain why I had to leave so suddenly."

She nodded. "Go on."

I tried to be brief and unemotional as I told her about the Mobil bombing and the fact that the NYPD Bomb Squad did not locate the bomb in our office after there was a bomb threat.

"I understand how you might be feeling. But let me assure you that this was different. Clearly, it was a prank phone call. There have been several lately...."

The words *There have been several lately* reverberated in my head. I could not believe what this woman said to me. She thinks that a threat could never be real, especially if they are repeated threats. It reminds me of the fable "The Boy Who Cried Wolf." It's the same apathetic response that people had in the violent '70s in NYC. There were so many threats that people ignored them until a bomb actually went off and people were killed.

How would she feel if her perception of a prank phone call turned into a bomb that went off in a classroom, killing several children?

"If we have to evacuate again and you leave, you will be written up. You have a responsibility to our students," she said.

She obviously does not understand how I feel about the NYPD Bomb Squad deciding that the building was safe, and then a bomb went off ten feet away from me and killed a man.

"Do you understand what I am saying?"

"I do," I responded. "You may have to write me up."

I luckily escaped death in 1977, but it could have been me. What are the chances that I would escape death if a bomb went off near me again?

I no longer felt safe in that school. I made a quick decision to resign without discussing it with my husband. It was a knee-jerk reaction, but when I did tell him, he said he understood and figured I could easily find another job. I decided to start a private practice, which was a good decision.

I thought that with my own practice, I would have control over where I was working and whether I could leave. This was the second time I had been confronted with workplace violence, and I wanted to be the one in control if it ever happened again. I thought the chances of it happening again were low, but my ever-constant fear for my safety caused me to make a career change that gave me more control. Or so I thought.

*   *   *

By the end of 1999, my new private practice in speech-language pathology was thriving. Even though news reports of terrorist acts reached my ears and continued to affect me as if I were a victim, on those high-anxiety days, I could call a client and reschedule if needed without giving a reason.

With my own private practice, I could concentrate on providing quality services instead of worrying about bomb threats and how administrators were or were not handling them. Although I had several contracts with school systems, most of my practice focused on adults in skilled nursing facilities or through home health agencies, many of whom had facial paralysis, weak throat muscles, and weak respiratory muscles that impacted their ability to communicate and swallow. I felt like there was more that I could do to help them.

There was some clinical evidence that massage to the head, neck, and chest muscles could positively affect speech and swallowing. So, to help my patients, I decided I needed formal training in massage therapy. I took one massage course and decided I didn't know enough about the techniques to be good at it. I chose to enroll in the Bancroft School of Massage in Worcester, Massachusetts and became a licensed massage therapist in 2000.

I never realized that giving and receiving massage would have such a significant impact on my ability to relax and, over time, process emotions. I received massages twice weekly when I was at Bancroft, and I exchanged massages with my classmate, Bonnie, every week after graduation. When I first started in massage school, my instructors told me that I had to get out of my head and into my hands. I was intent on letting my mind determine what strokes to use and how to work on someone. When you use that mechanical approach, massage doesn't feel that good to the person on the table. I needed to learn to be intuitive—to let my hands feel the tissue and let them decide what the body needed. As a practitioner, your best work happens when you feel the body's energy on your table and let your intuition guide you. This was so hard for me, but I got better and better with every massage I provided. I got myself into a very grounded state when I performed a massage and even more so when I received it. I do think that with every massage I provided and every massage I received, a small part of the cellular barrier concealing my emotions was massaged away.

By January 2001, I had opened a massage therapy practice in addition to my private practice in speech-language pathology. I'd see three to four clients weekly for massage in a small office attached to my home. This provided extra money for vacations or my dog show hobby. Although my husband worked as a machinist, our primary source of income was from my private practice in speech-language pathology.

✳   ✳   ✳

On September 11, 2001, I was consulting in the school system in Winchendon, Massachusetts. As I walked through the library to get to a student's classroom, I noticed several teachers standing around the widescreen TV that was suspended from the ceiling. I moved closer, then stopped short as I heard the words *terrorist attack.*

Oh no, no, no. This cannot be happening. Are they watching a terrorist attack on television?

I knew I shouldn't look, but I couldn't help myself. I needed to know what was happening. I took several slow steps forward and looked up at the television. Reporters were talking about Al Qaeda terrorist attacks in New York City. They stated that terrorists hijacked four commercial airlines and crashed two planes into the Twin Towers of the World Trade Center.

New York City is four hours away.

The third plane struck the Pentagon, and the fourth plane crashed in Pennsylvania.

I looked away from the TV as I could not process any further information. I felt numb and paralyzed by the news. I couldn't move my feet. I felt vulnerable and in danger.

Tears were streaming down my face, and I felt like everyone was staring at me (but they weren't). This was the first terrorist attack I became aware of since the Mobil bombing. Other people were in disbelief, and although they expressed sadness, they would never understand the extent of the emotional damage to survivors and families of victims. The events of 9/11 brought back terrorism as a reality to me and all the emotional mess that came with it.

At that very moment, I felt compassion for the people involved and anger at the terrorists. This was the first time I recall having those feelings. Up until this moment, I had been emotionally numb. I also felt emotionally exhausted and sick to my stomach. I couldn't think about or focus on anything.

I left for the day, went home, and found myself again fully clothed in bed. My husband was not at all supportive and told me he was leaving for a few days to stay with friends. This time, I stayed in bed for a couple of days until I could think clearly. I couldn't get over the fact that this was my third experience with terrorism (real or threat) while I was at work and that my husband would leave me to deal with this alone.

Why is terrorism following me?

A once-in-a-lifetime experience with threats of violence or terrorism was more than enough...but this was the third, and unfortunately, not the last.

CHAPTER 10

THE DOG LADY WHO LIVED IN THE WOODS

In 2005, when I turned fifty, my knees were starting to creak, and I had osteoporosis and the beginnings of osteoarthritis. I realized I had slowly replaced much of my running time with my hobby of breeding and showing dogs. My husband, who used to take interest in the dogs by helping me show them, had become very critical of them. He had become critical of me and everything I did. He frequently came home late or was gone for a few days with no explanation. Then, one day, he packed a suitcase and said, "I'm leaving you." Soon after, my friends saw him in public with another woman.

I became a single dog lady in 2007.

My dogs were always there for me and faithful, unlike my second husband. His frequent late nights and trips away now made sense. He had been seeing other women throughout our marriage. He called me "cold" and "uncaring." He said I wasn't emotional enough and was too logical. Maybe that was true, but he never mentioned he was unhappy, instead lying to me throughout our marriage. Maybe my lack of emotion and poor intuition interfered with my ability to recognize red flags and try to resolve them. But again, the responsibility to make a marriage work does not fall on one person.

Our divorce was final in 2007, and I resolved that relationships just weren't going to work for me. I was too disconnected from myself to be connected to someone else. I could choose a good show dog, but not the right man. At least, that's what I had convinced myself of at the time.

After my divorce, I still had my private practice in speech-language pathology, a part-time massage therapy practice, and the dog kennel. I had seven Boston Terriers that I cared for, trained, and took into the show ring. It was easier to be around dogs than people. Dogs don't judge. They listen to you and provide unconditional love. I loved having multiple dogs around me all the time. They were my family. They accepted every part of me and helped me stay in the present rather than living in the past.

In 2008, I moved to a different house three miles away for a fresh start with more room for the dogs and me. It was set back in the woods, away from civilization and everything I perceived as a threat, such as crowds and public places. I enjoyed my solitude and loved to look out the window to admire the birch trees in the woods behind my house. One afternoon, the phone rang as I sat in the kitchen watching the birds flit through the birch trees. I grabbed the phone receiver from the wall to answer it. I heard an unfamiliar male voice on the other end when I put the receiver to my ear.

"Hello. Is this Christi Scarpino?" the voice asked.

I wondered if this was one of my ex's friends calling to aggravate me or dig for information. I quickly decided to respond, being prepared to hang up the phone.

"Yes," I responded.

"You probably don't remember me, but this is Bill Maus. I met you in 1988 when you were a passenger on the American Hawaii Cruise ship U.S.S. Constitution."

Whoa...What is going on here? He's the engineer who promised to call me. I felt my hand tighten on the receiver as I felt confused but also curious about this phone call.

"I do remember you" was all I could manage to say.

"That's good," he said. "I know it's been a while, but I lost your phone number. I was going through some old paperwork recently, and I found a slip of paper with your name and number on it."

"Oh...kay....It's only been close to twenty years. Why are you even calling me?" I said as I sat down at the kitchen table.

"I said I'd call you, and I keep my promises. I want to apologize for not calling you sooner. I feel really bad about it."

I thought he ghosted me, but he calls me nearly twenty years later and apologizes? Who does that? I didn't even know what to say in response.

"Thank you for not hanging up on me. I'm glad I found you. Soooo...what have you been up to?"

I gave Bill a condensed version of the last twenty years of my life. I learned that he was no longer on cruise ships but was chief engineer on other types of ships and traveled all over the world. He returned to his home state of New Jersey once or twice per year between his jobs at sea. We talked for an hour or so, and then I just had to ask.

"Why did you call me?" My head and heart were in conflict. An old romantic interest presented itself just as I became available after my divorce.

Without hesitation, he said, "You're a good person. I feel like I owe you an explanation and an apology."

My exhaled breath was full of relief. I didn't want to open the door to a new romance. I was very happy with my life as a dog lady who lived in the woods.

We ended our phone conversation, and Bill asked me if he could continue to call me whenever he got home from sea. I politely agreed. He was an interesting person, and I liked talking to him. I doubted that he would continue to call, but he continued to call me frequently over the next ten years.

*   *   *

I had settled further into my identity as a dog person, which made me feel normal. Being labeled a dog person satisfied my need for identity. There was more to my identity than that, but I hadn't found it yet, and this was good for the time being.

My interest in dogs expanded as I wanted to do more training and performance competitions. I loved my Boston

Terriers, but they were not that interested in obedience training and competition, which was what I wanted to do. I decided to look for a medium-sized dog that required minimal grooming and that had a serious work ethic.

One day, while showing one of my Bostons, I saw these lively red dogs in the next ring. When I came out of the ring, I started talking to the people who were showing these red dogs. I discovered they were Nova Scotia Duck Tolling Retrievers, commonly called Tollers. Over the next few months, I met with breeders and learned all about the breed. They are intelligent, medium-sized dogs who are energetic and love to work. They do not require extensive grooming, but they do shed. (I didn't care because that's why we have vacuums.)

All the boxes were checked, and I got my first Toller, Turner. He fit in well with the seven Boston Terriers already living with me.

Turner was what we call "a lot of dog"—more dog than I was prepared for. He had such high energy and drive that he was hard for me to control. One obedience instructor told me to find another dog, which only made me work harder with Turner.

I've never been a person who gives up easily. I have been described as dedicated, determined, and focused by my friends, family, and colleagues. Once I start a task, I like to finish it, no matter how long it takes. I don't give up on my dogs, other people, and especially myself.

I still was not satisfied with who I had become. Flash-backs and panic attacks continued, but I was determined to find a way to be free of them. Similarly, I would find a way to change Turner's behavior and transform him into the performance dog I wanted. I worked hard with him, and he eventually turned into my service dog—although he was never trained to be one.

Turner and I were inseparable. He was my heart dog, companion, and protector. Dogs are good at reading non-verbal signals. I think Turner understood my emotional states and recognized my anxiety better than I did; he was always there to help me. I could mask my emotions in front of people but not to Turner. He gave me strength when I needed it most.

Turner was a dog who liked to assert himself and do what he wanted, not necessarily what I wanted him to do. His behavior was what we call in the dog world "reactive." Certain things (triggers) would cause him to bark and lunge, and there were people who were afraid of him because of it. I suppose we were both reactive since I responded to my own triggers. I had to watch his nonverbal behavior every minute to keep him calm and prevent him from escalating to the scary-acting Turner. However, he watched my non-verbal behavior as much as I watched him. It's amazing to me that he and I could read each other and manage each other's behavior, although we both could not control some of our own behaviors. He was always watching me out of the corner of his eye and would intervene if he felt he needed to.

There were several times when Turner warned me that I was about to have a flashback or helped me navigate those days when I just wasn't emotionally right. For example,

I was lying on the couch one day, scrolling on my phone. I started reading a news report about violence, which was (and still is) a trigger for me. Even though I was aware that I was intentionally exposing myself to a trigger, I could not make myself stop reading. My heart was pounding in my chest, and I could feel my breathing become more rapid and shallow. I was frozen—until a forty-two-pound dog jumped up on the couch and sat on my chest, knocking the phone out of my hand with his paw. As my phone crashed onto the hardwood floor, Turner laid himself down on my body and put his head on my shoulder. There he was, providing deep pressure to calm me after he stopped me from reading something that upset me.

I trained Turner to compete in American Kennel Club (AKC) obedience trials. Training him for the obedience ring and helping him attain his Utility Dog title was bumpy because he was always on the alert for my safety and did not want any unfamiliar person or dog to approach me. He would never leave my side unless I allowed him to or if I was having a rough emotional day.

Rainy days were tough for me. On the day of the bombing, it was pouring when I was evacuated from buildings several times, so rain remained a trigger thirty years later. I felt lethargic and depressed when it rained, but I usually managed to drag myself through the day. Some days, I couldn't even get out of bed.

One rainy Saturday in November, Turner was entered into an obedience trial at the Eastern States Exposition Center in Springfield, Massachusetts. We had to get up at 4:00 a.m. to get ready with enough time to make the two-hour trip to the venue. As the alarm clock rang, I could hear the heavy downpour of rain on the roof. I started to feel the pressure all around me, and I felt like I was gasping for air. It was hard to breathe.

Maybe I should skip the obedience trial today, I thought as I pulled the covers over my head.

My thought of skipping the trial ceased when Turner leaped onto the bed and plopped himself down on my chest. His positioning forced me to take a deep breath into my diaphragm. The deep pressure of his body on my core had a calming effect. As I lowered the covers from my face, I saw a happy dog face staring at me as if to say, "It's time to get up. We have plans for today, and I'm ready." The alarm was still going strong, but Turner slapped it with his paw before I could get my hand to the off button.

We both got up, and I let all the dogs out and fed them. As I quickly sipped my cup of coffee, I reviewed my positive affirmations and to-do list for the day. Turner sat next to the door, by his leash, ready to leave, "Okay, boy, let's go!" I said, trying to sound enthusiastic. We went into the garage, I opened the car hatch, and Turner jumped into his crate. Off we went on the long drive to Springfield in the pouring rain.

During the drive, I was fighting with my intrusive thoughts.

I can't eliminate these bad feelings no matter how hard I try.

I want to go back to bed and stay there forever.

I don't want to see any people.

I've got to snap out of this for my dog.

After we got to the Big E, I got Turner settled in his crate and waited for our number, 207, to be called to enter the obedience ring.

About thirty minutes later, the ring steward called, "Number 207, get ready...you're next."

Turner and I warmed up for our obedience ring by taking a five-minute walk around the ring area. He never stopped looking at me as we walked, but my eyes were drawn to all the umbrellas on the sidelines. Yellow umbrella on the left...Red umbrella on the right...Small black umbrella hanging from the chair...Umbrellas open and drying just outside of the grooming area.

On the inside, I was feeling shaky, hearing the rain on the roof of the building and seeing all the umbrellas. However, on the outside, I needed to exude confidence. I needed to appear focused and calm. Perhaps I looked that way to the people around me, but Turner saw right through it. I took a deep breath and stepped into the ring with Turner.

"Good morning," said the judge. "This is your heeling exercise. Are you ready?"

"Yes," I replied, definitely not feeling ready for anything.

Turner and I completed this and several other exercises well, and now it was time for directed jumping. In this exercise, the dog sits by your side, and you send them away from you to the end of the ring where the dog sits facing you. Then, according to the judge's directions, you signal your dog to go over a specific jump on the way back to you. This was one of Turner's favorite exercises.

We positioned ourselves for the exercise, and the judge said, "This is the directed jumping exercise. Are you ready?"

Turner was supposed to look straight out as we had practiced many times, but he still would not take his eyes off me. He moved closer, so his right shoulder rubbed against my left leg. It was very odd that he was leaning into me.

"Turner, this is a go-out. Look far," I said nervously, placing my flat hand next to his head as a cue. Turner was still looking up at me as I became more aware of the sound of the torrential downpour on the roof. I felt like the room was closing in on me, yet I had to send my dog to the end of the ring.

How long had we been standing still at the end of the ring?

"Send your dog," said the judge.

"Go out!" I said to Turner in my most enthusiastic voice. But he sat there, looking at me, and did not move. I tried a second time. "Go out!" Turner responded by leaning closer to my body and not taking a step forward.

"Exercise finished!" said the judge. "That's too bad because he did great on the other exercises." This was a polite way of saying Turner had passed everything else, but his refusal to leave me caused him to fail this exercise.

The ring steward brought me Turner's leash, I hooked him up, and we exited the ring. We failed the trial, but Turner didn't fail me. He saw through my masked feelings and leaned into me, giving me the deep physical pressure I needed to calm my nervous system. He refused to leave my side. He knew I needed him nearby because I was reacting to the trigger of the rain. Turner was learning to manage me as much as I was learning to manage him.

In addition to obedience, I trained Turner in hunting/retrieving. Although I did not hunt, Turner loved retrieving so much that I could not deny him the opportunity to hunt and retrieve in structured settings, such as training and hunt tests. Again, he was always at my side. We were a great team at hunt tests as long as the weather was sunny, and I was in a good frame of mind.

Around the same time, we entered the seasoned hunting retriever test at Granite State Hunting Retriever Club. I was a member of this club and excited because we had trained hard and were ready to compete on our home turf. The weather forecast showed the test day as being sunny and warm, but it was pouring rain on the morning of the test. Rain usually triggered intrusive thoughts that made it difficult for me to concentrate and participate in anything. I wasn't happy about running my dog in the rain, but I was sure glad that I hadn't volunteered to help at the test. Members were required to work at one event per year, and I had already met my obligation.

Great. I get to spend the day outside in the pouring rain. I would rather stay in bed, but I think I can do this. I can rise above my rain trigger.

I did not want to disappoint the people who had been helping me train my dog. It was our chance to shine in a more advanced test setup. So, off I went with Turner.

The day was a disaster. The rain didn't stop and neither did the pressure in my head. I took Turner to the line to retrieve, and he refused to leave my side. A "no go" is a failure, so we returned to my car to dry off.

Why did I think I could run Turner in the rain? I am not as strong as I think I am.

Tears streamed down my face. A knock on my driver's side window interrupted my negative thoughts about myself. I looked up to see two people standing there, arms folded, staring at me intently. I rolled down the window.

"Hey, get out of your car and come help at the started test. You're done running your dog, and we need you to help," said the man. The woman stood there silently next to him, nodding in agreement.

"I'm not feeling well," I said, showing my tear-stained face as I looked up at him. "I think I just need to go home."

"Well," he said in an admonishing tone of voice. "You are not living up to your obligation to help as a club member. What kind of person are you, anyway?"

His comment took me aback, and I just wanted to smack him upside the head. How dare this man, who hardly knew me, insinuate that I was lazy? How dare he try to shame me into helping? How dare he not recognize that I was very upset? I certainly wasn't going to try to defend myself or explain why I was sitting in my car. I hadn't volunteered to help at this event. Wouldn't his time be better spent helping the club instead of chastising me? It wasn't worth the time and effort to allow myself to get more upset or defensive. The best thing I could do was to roll up my window, start the car, and drive home.

Once home, I changed into dry clothes, and Turner and I snuggled beneath the warm covers of my bed until the rain stopped.

I must thank Turner for getting me through rough times and saving me from myself. He was my main reason for getting up in the morning. I trained him to get field and obedience titles and showed him to his AKC Championship. I am very proud of his titles, but his role as my service dog and companion meant the most to me. He alerted me when a panic attack was coming on. He wouldn't let me stay in bed depressed. He'd jump on the bed and dump his slimy toys on my chest until I got up. He made me laugh. He never left my side. He just did what came naturally, and I am such a lucky woman to have him in my life. Turner was with me until 2022, when he passed at the age of fifteen.

My life has continued with dogs as companions and performance dogs. I slowly phased out having Boston Terriers, but now I have three Tollers—Nadia, her son Alden, and Encore. I love my dogs to pieces, but there will never be another Turner. He truly was my heart dog...my soulmate.

My life with Turner increased my awareness of the onset of panic attacks and flashbacks, enabling me to manage them and sometimes avert having them at all. I became able to recognize the early signs of my anxiety and panic attacks and deal with them before they interrupted my ability to function. Although this was good, it also was detrimental.

Along with my increased self-awareness came an increased perception of emotions. The numbness that I had grown accustomed to transformed into emotions that came with an overwhelming intensity. Sometimes, I felt incredibly sad for no apparent reason, and sometimes, I would feel like there was an emotional pain inside me that could not get out. I did not have control over these feelings, which became a problem for me.

CHAPTER 11

YOU'RE AS GOOD AS YOU'RE GOING TO GET

I'd get a phone call from Bill every six to nine months. Our conversations were pretty neutral, yet I wondered why he continued to call me. I'd always ask why, and he'd always answer, "Because you're such a good person." I just thought it was an odd reason to call someone you met once over two decades ago.

It was in early June 2011 when he called me from Boston. His ship was in dry dock, and he asked if I would come to Boston to meet him for lunch that coming Sunday. That was only ninety minutes by train, and I had nothing else planned, so I agreed.

As the day drew closer, I thought, *What on earth was I even thinking when I accepted his invitation? Does he want to see me because I'm a good person, or is there more to this?*

I didn't know what to think, but I knew I wasn't in a good emotional place to be in a relationship. At fifty-six years old, I was still figuring out who I was and what I wanted out of life. I needed to keep my life simple. So, I had a solution. I sorted through my jewelry box until I found the diamond ring I had purchased several years earlier to celebrate my successful private practice. I would pretend to be engaged.

Sunday came, and I drove to Fitchburg and caught the train to North Station in Boston. I dressed casually, with minimal make-up and jewelry, except for the diamond ring on my left ring finger. I figured if Bill had any romantic ideas, the diamond ring would send the message that I wasn't available.

In all our conversations, I had never shared anything about the bombing or what I had been dealing with. I had omitted that part of my life to appear "normal." I also didn't want to burden him with my emotional baggage. It was better left unsaid since I wanted to be acquaintances from the past and leave it at that.

Bill and I recognized one another in North Station. Our greeting consisted of a quick smile and handshake, which felt a little awkward but safe. The weather was warm and sunny, and we spent the afternoon walking the Freedom Trail and having lunch in an outdoor café. We talked about our families and our jobs.

After a few hours, I glanced at my train schedule and mentioned that I needed to get going.

"I'll walk you back to North Station," Bill said. But, if you need to use the bathroom, you can use the one in my hotel room before you go."

No, no, no, I thought. *The last place I want to go is your hotel room.*

"No thanks," I said as I rubbed my cheek with my left hand, making my diamond ring quite visible. "I need to get back home to let out my dogs and feed them."

We returned to North Station and found the platform for my train home.

We stared at each other for a moment,

"It was great seeing you again," I said. "Thank you for lunch and a lovely afternoon."

Bill took a step forward, and before I knew it, he gave me a quick hug. To me, it was an electric hug. Bells and whistles and alarms went off inside me. It was the same feeling I had when we were together in 1988. I couldn't deny the intensity of the butterflies and gushy feeling I had when he touched me.

"Bye," he said. "I'll call you."

I turned away and walked quickly to my train. I got into the first available car and sat down. Looking out the window, I could still see Bill standing there.

Why were my eyes tearing up a bit?
Should I have kissed him?

Oddly enough, I wished I *had* kissed him. But then, I was also pretending to be an engaged woman, so that would have been entirely inappropriate. I reminded myself that I needed to ignore those intense feelings during the hug because a relationship was not in the cards for me right now. I felt so conflicted between what I was feeling and what was reality. The presence of those romantic feelings surprised me. I told myself I was fantasizing.

He probably wasn't interested in me. I had given him plenty of opportunities to say I was still a romantic interest, but he insisted that I was just a good person and friend. I wasn't good in relationships with men anyway. I shut my eyes and napped on the train ride home.

✶   ✶   ✶

Over the next year, I noticed that I was starting to feel emotions, mostly happiness, sadness, and empathy. Up to this point, I felt numb and void of emotion unless being triggered. I seldom cried. I seldom laughed. Dealing with a lack of emotion for the past thirty-five years was the programming I was used to; pretending to feel a certain emotion in a social situation had become a way of life.

Yet, in that year, I noticed that I would become sad and depressed upon hearing about other acts of violence, including terrorist attacks. Just reading or hearing about terrorism re-ignited my flashbacks and physical symptoms, but now I was flooded with sadness for the people involved. I avoided the media as much as possible to avoid triggering news, but news of terrorism always reached me...maybe even easier than weather reports.

On April 15, 2013, I was providing speech therapy to a stroke patient in their home. In the next room, which was still viewable from where I was, the patient's husband turned on the TV to watch the Boston Marathon on low volume. I must admit that due to my running background, my attention was diverted from my patient to the TV screen. I noticed that something was going on.

I could see crowds of people and heard the words *terrorist* and *bombing*. I became fixated on the screen only to see a live news report from Boston about a bomb that had exploded during the marathon, injuring and killing people. I could feel myself panic as my heart beat into my throat and my breathing became rapid. This was too close to home. Terrorism was only ninety minutes away. I could feel myself starting to be transported back to the Mobil bombing, but I was able to stop it before I got there.

I got stuck somewhere in between a flashback and reality. I didn't feel like I was physically in the employment office as I did in previous flashbacks. I knew I was in a patient's home, and I also knew that I was starting to feel the physical symptoms from the explosion at Mobil. The nausea and pressure on my head had started. This was a moment of progress for me as I recognized my trauma responses early and could manage myself in a socially acceptable manner.

I was able to end my patient's therapy session, albeit abruptly. I didn't give a reason. I just finished the session a little earlier than usual. I don't recall driving home, which was not unusual due to my short-term memory loss, but I did arrive home safely. I took the rest of the day off from work and went to bed. I don't know how long I stayed there, but as I touched my necklace, I knew I was safe.

The logical part of my brain knew that a terrorist was not going to come to my home in Ashburnham. But the emotional part was not in agreement. *Boston is only ninety minutes away, and terrorism is back. It's following me. I'll never feel safe.* I was overcome with these intrusive thoughts about my safety, and now I was worried about the people in the Boston Marathon. *How would survivors cope? How would family and friends react and cope? No one deserves to live through what I have lived through. I feel so bad for them. They will have to live with this experience for the rest of their lives.*

I noticed that with my newfound empathy, my emotional switch sometimes turned on, and the emotional floodgates opened up over "nothing." I would often feel overcome with deep sadness with uncontrollable episodes of sobbing when viewing things like comical YouTube videos, a beautiful sunrise or sunset, and even a newly blooming flower in the garden.

I can remember lying in bed, watching the season twelve auditions for *American Idol.* I was a big fan of *American Idol* and always enjoyed watching the audition performances. Not in 2013. I bawled my eyes out when a singer was good. I bawled when the audition wasn't good. It didn't matter. I just cried and cried. The contrast between feeling few emotions for many years and feeling intense emotions all the time was too much for me to handle.

✶　✶　✶

Since the Mobil bombing, I had been seeing Dr. Siebel for cognitive behavioral therapy (CBT) fairly consistently for thirty years. I took a break from treatment from about 2008 to 2013 because I felt I was handling my day-to-day life well. In 2013, I felt the need to return to therapy because my intense feelings made me feel more broken. I felt there was more to fix and unravel inside myself if I wanted to feel like I was a whole person who had control over herself and her life. Not being able to understand or control my own emotions was unsettling, so I decided to go back to therapy and see Dr. Siebel.

I saw Dr. Siebel for a few sessions to discuss the unpredictable deluge of emotions I was feeling and my inability to control them. I was so overcome with the onslaught of emotions that it prevented me from concentrating and getting things done. Staying busy was still one of my primary coping mechanisms, but the emotional overload made that problematic. Being overly emotional kept me from being productive, which only increased my anxiety. I felt lost in a mountain of tears. I also expressed that sometimes I felt actual pain in my head and my chest before and after the crying episodes.

My interpretation of my conversations with Dr. Siebel was that my newly appearing emotions were a good thing and a step towards healing. Maybe that was true, but it didn't feel like healing. It made me feel out of control and more broken. Dr. Seibel seemed pleased with my progress and told me I had improved to the point that I didn't need any more therapy. Her words resounded loudly in my head.

You should be pleased with your progress. You are ready to be discharged.

The effects of the bombing will never go away. You will have to use your strategies to cope.

My brain's translation was *This is as good as you're going to get. Accept yourself with your problems, compensate, and live your life.*

This was unacceptable.

I did not think I had progressed as far as I could go. I couldn't believe that the influx of emotions after feeling "dead" for so many years was normal. I wanted to understand it. Fix it. Make myself better. There were still missing pieces. I had been receiving CBT for years, and for years, I thought it helped. I didn't think I needed anything else, so I didn't pursue other treatment. I wanted to make more improvements. If cognitive therapy wasn't going to help me find those pieces of myself, I decided to explore different modalities for self-discovery.

✶   ✶   ✶

After my therapy in 2013, I was on a mission to self-heal. I pursued many avenues to help me deal with my emotions and my continued physical responses: self-help books, meditation, tarot card readings, movement therapy, crystal bowl sound baths, craniosacral therapy, acupuncture, and massage. The method that helped me the most was massage.

In 2014, I was still searching for answers for my emotional release. As a massage therapist, I realized that there is a mind-body connection and that emotions can be trapped in the body. This can result in physical pain and increased emotions such as anxiety, sadness, and anger. Massage can catalyze the body to release these negative emotions, and the client can become emotional on the massage table. I had seen this happen with a few of my clients who cried during treatment. You can't make yourself have a release. It just happens when you are ready. I didn't know it yet, but it was time for me to experience this release.

I made an appointment with a different local massage practitioner named Jean. At Jean's office, I filled out a case history form and indicated that the purpose of my massage was for relaxation. She showed me to a small room, suggested that I undress to the level of my comfort, and lie on my back on the massage table.

Jean left the room so I could get undressed and get situated under the sheets.

"Are you all set?" she asked as she knocked softly on the door.

"Yes, I am," I responded as I mentally prepared myself to be touched. Since the bombing, I had become very sensitive to being touched, particularly on my feet. I needed to tell her that. When someone touched my feet, it felt like someone was scratching me with their pointy fingernails down my spine. It hurt. I'm not sure why. In the Chinese practice of reflexology, specific points of the feet correspond to different organs and parts of the body. I wondered if my internal system was so dysregulated that it couldn't decipher or organize the tactile input. I also wondered if my feet were holding onto trauma from walking in the bloody six-inch platform shoes on the day of the bombing.

"Please don't touch my feet. They are very sensitive. It actually feels painful to me."

"Thank you for telling me," she said as she cradled my head in her hands and gently tucked her fingers into my neck muscles. "I will communicate with you during the massage to see how you are feeling. You can also tell me that you want more or less pressure at any time. Now, take a deep breath."

I followed her direction and took several deep breaths, falling into a deep state of relaxation. I appreciated the firmness and intention of her effleurage strokes as I was transported to another level of consciousness.

"How are you feeling?" she asked after she completed working on my legs, skipping my feet as promised. "Do you mind if I work on your abdomen? Not everyone likes abdominal work, but I thought I would ask."

I didn't usually have my abdomen massaged, but for some reason, I agreed.

"Sure. Go ahead."

She re-draped my body so she could access my abdomen without exposing my breasts and started making long, deep strokes across my core, which felt amazing to me. In massage lingo, she was working on my hara, the body's energy center. It is central to emotional and mental stability.

As I lay there, feeling her strokes, my stomach felt increasingly warm, but not in a good way. Something was bubbling up inside me, and I had a flashing vision of hot lava, which startled me.

"Are you feeling OK? Jean asked, noticing that my breathing had become a bit shallow.

Just as I responded that I thought I was good, my body stiffened.

I cried out as I visualized a black tornado swirling out of my stomach. I arched my back and groaned as Jean lifted her hands and stepped away from the table.

I felt a rush of energy leaving my body from my left foot.

"Ohhhhhh," I sighed as my body sunk back into the massage table.

I regained my composure and looked at Jean, who was still a couple of feet from the table. "What was that? It felt like a hot mess just left my body. Did you feel anything?"

Jean stepped closer to me and said, "You just had a huge release of negative energy. They were emotions that weren't serving you, and you let them go. That's so wonderful."

Jean completed the massage to the back part of my body in the time left. As I lay on my stomach, I tried to process what had happened. I felt calmer, and it felt like a bunch of bad stuff inside me was gone. That was the only emotional release I have had from massage, but it was powerful enough for me to believe that emotions are stored in your body. It was powerful enough for me to understand that negative emotions do not serve you. It was powerful enough to make me want to figure out how to release the remainder of the unprocessed emotions in my body.

But I have to admit—this massage experience freaked me out. I am sure that the intuition I developed as a massage therapist increased my awareness of my body and maybe even my feelings. My emotional and physical responses to life continued to be present and ever-changing. I had become more aware of how I was feeling.

My awareness of my feelings was both a curse and a blessing. I was still overcome with emotion at times, but I also was less tolerant of my emotional reactions and could not conceal or mask my feelings from myself. Although I had a big emotional release from the massage with Jean, it was obvious that my body was still harboring negative energy and emotions that needed to be released. I was still crying at the drop of a hat. I still experienced the buzzing in my head every day when I woke up. There were still some things that triggered flashbacks and nightmares and plenty of things that I avoided because they triggered me.

Although I had experienced a release of negative energy and emotion from Jean's massage, I started to feel a nagging, sharp pain in my head and left collarbone every day. Perhaps the massage released enough blockage so that I was beginning to feel more emotional and even physical pain in my body. I felt like something was stuck in there that wanted to get out. I could not get rid of it. I tried all the tools in my toolbox, and this nagging emotional pain was always there. I used to be able to mask these responses by acting like a superwoman and keeping myself busy every second of the day. I had been using the masking and avoidance strategies for forty years, and I was tired of them.

Masking also wasn't as effective as it once was. I could no longer cover up my feelings and pain by ignoring them. I wanted to get rid of the emotional and physical pain once and for all. It was hard for me to share my pain with anyone, and I did not think returning to cognitive therapy would be helpful.

I decided to confide in my friend, Bonnie, a person who was aware of my trauma but also the person I exchanged weekly massages with. I knew she would listen with compassion and without judgment. And so she did, and she told me about EMDR, a therapy that would turn out to be life-changing for me. EMDR turned out to be what I needed. I am forever grateful to Bonnie for listening to and supporting me through the process. She was the first friend who understood my pain and helped me through it.

CHAPTER 12

NOT BROKEN ANY MORE

Developed by psychologist Francine Shapiro, PhD, EMDR stands for eye movement desensitization and reprocessing. EMDR is a process that provides a way to be free from disturbing thoughts and memories. I wasn't sure if this was something that would help me, but it was a technique used to treat disturbing memories of trauma that I suffered from.

Dr. Shapiro likens the process of EMDR to the process of digestion. As the body physically processes the food you ingest, the mind emotionally processes experiences. To be emotionally healthy, the mind processes upsetting experiences so the person can move on. When a person experiences a severe trauma, these upsetting experiences and painful memories get stuck, causing full-blown flashbacks so intense that it feels like they are reliving the event. The person gets "stuck" in that past experience. They cannot

forget it. They can't free themselves from it. Their perceptions of the terrible event (what they saw, heard, smelled,
and felt) are stuck in their present experiences. The awful-
ness of the past blasts itself into the present.

I thought that description could have been about me.
When triggered, I could feel the pressure around my body.
My head felt like it was being squeezed so hard that my
brain would come out of my ears; I could smell and taste
gunpowder and breathe the thick air. Sometimes, I would
see blood on the walls and floor in front of me. Although
these sensory experiences seemed real to me, they were
unprocessed perceptions that persisted in the form of nightmares, flashbacks, and intrusive thoughts. My primary coping mechanism was avoidance of triggers by staying busy
and isolating myself. These actions were not always possible. I needed something else to be free.

After learning more about EMDR, I wondered if it
would be worth it and if I could even do it. I'd have to open
up about my trauma with a new therapist almost forty years
after the trauma occurred. I would have to discuss painful
events with a new person. Would the psychologist simply
dismiss my concerns after having so much previous therapy? Would EMDR even be appropriate after such a long
time? Would I be a good candidate? Did I have a diagnosis
that would warrant the treatment? Going to a new therapist
would be the only way to find out.

I started my search for a qualified EMDR therapist
in 2015. I wanted to find a therapist who was a certified
EMDR practitioner who had worked with people who

lived through a traumatic experience. After a month of background checking, I made an appointment with Dr. Neil Castronovo, a psychologist in Worcester, Massachusetts.

I was filled with excitement and apprehension as I drove to his office. It is always hard for me to tell my story. Most of the time, whenever I opened my mouth to tell my story, I was met with the sound of crickets. People, even psychologists, didn't know what to say. It makes an uncomfortable situation even worse for me. I was ready for it today. But it didn't happen with Dr. Castronovo.

I felt comfortable with him from the moment I stepped into his office. As we chatted, I discovered he was a fellow New Yorker, familiar with the time, setting, and even some details of the Mobil bombing. He encouraged me to tell my story in detail.

I recounted the events of August 3, 1977, as best as I could, not making eye contact with Dr. Castronovo. It was easier for me to look away, but with an occasional glance in his direction, I could see that he was attentive and taking notes.

I sat up tall and let out a big sigh.

"I am broken," my voice trembled. "I feel like I'm pieces of shattered glass all over the table. None of the pieces fit together, and some of them are missing." I took another deep breath and pressed my fingers around my teardrop necklace. "Those glass pieces are jabbing at me all the time. I can't stand it."

Dr. Castronovo paused his notetaking, looked up at me, and said, "You mentioned on the telephone that you are interested in EMDR. What would you like it to do for you?"

I wasn't expecting that question. I thought the answer was obvious, but I paused a minute to think and quietly replied, "I want to get rid of the pain once and for all. I have tried all the tools and techniques I have learned from therapies over the past thirty-seven years, but I can't get rid of it."

I reached up and touched my necklace again, pressing the ruby teardrop between my thumb and index finger.

"I'm tired of fighting it, running from it, and distracting myself from it. I want to wake up and feel like an integrated person. I want to feel peace and be calm, focused, and centered."

I exhaled loudly, and my hand dropped into my lap.

Dr. Castronovo continued to take case history information, and then he said, "Tell me how you feel during the summer months, particularly around the anniversary date of the terrorist attack."

Another unexpected question. Why did he suspect I might have difficulty during that time? What did he know about me that I didn't tell him?

"Well," I said, with tears in my eyes, "it starts at the beginning of July every year,"

"What starts?"

"The nightmares. The flashbacks. I feel nervous all the time, and I can't concentrate. I stop eating and sleeping. I relive the bombing over and over again. It's like I'm in the Mobil office every day."

With my right hand, I grabbed my necklace and twisted it until it dug into my neck.

"How long does this last?"

I released my grip on my necklace so I could speak. "Usually until the end of August."

"That's called an anniversary reaction," he said very matter of factly. "It is very common for people who have experienced a severe trauma and have PTSD."

I could feel my heart beating in my throat.

"What? 'PTSD'?" This was the first time someone had mentioned that term to me.

"Yes, you've been experiencing PTSD for a long time."

I had never heard of post-traumatic stress disorder. I had many questions about this diagnosis that was new to me. From our conversation during that session, I learned that PTSD was not an official diagnosis until 1980, when it was included in the American Psychiatric Association's *Diagnostic and Statistical Manual of Mental Disorders* (*DSM-II*). At that time, it was considered an anxiety disorder that was related to war veterans. The diagnosis wasn't regarded as applying to civilians who had not been in war.

There were several revisions of the *DSM*'s criteria for the diagnosis of PTSD. Still, it wasn't until 2013 in the *DSM-5* that it was considered to be related to trauma and stress instead of anxiety. For a very long time, I thought people were withholding information from me and avoiding the issue of my mental illness. Now, I know there was a reason that it wasn't explained to me and why some of the therapists I saw did not seem to understand how to work with me.

"Therapy has obviously helped you, but it seems you are still looking for a way to stop the nightmares and flashbacks," Dr. Castronovo said. "Have I got that right?"

"Yes, that, and I want to stop the nagging pain I have in these three places," I said, pointing to my collarbone, my throat, and the right side of my head.

"It feels like something is poking my insides with a stick in those places. Nobody seems to believe me."

I sat up straight in the chair and looked Dr. Castronovo in the eyes. "Do you think EMDR can help me? Do you think you can help me?"

"Yes," he said. "It's worth a try. I can't guarantee results, but there is considerable evidence that EMDR can help people with your symptoms."

Our session time was running out, so I made another appointment to see Dr. Castronovo in a week. Further discussion about EMDR and my PTSD would be postponed until my next session.

During the week between sessions, I found out as much as I could about PTSD. I spent my evenings reading the *DSM-5* and seeing how well my symptoms fit into the description. First, the person must have been exposed to a traumatic event that is not typical for humans to experience. The type of trauma could be war and combat, violence and abuse, natural disaster and mass violence. The person must also witness or experience a life-threatening event. A terrorist attack met that criterion.

Next, I learned that there are four categories of symptoms characteristic of PTSD, and a person must exhibit a certain number of symptoms within each category. I was astonished to find out that I showed several of the symptoms in each category.

The first category involves exhibiting unwanted or upsetting memories that cause the person to relive the event. Examples include nightmares, flashbacks, emotional distress after being exposed to reminders of the trauma (also called triggers), and physical reactions in response to triggers. I checked all the boxes in this category.

The second category of symptoms includes avoiding things that remind the person of the trauma. I avoided crowds, television, newspapers, movies, and magazines. I kept a very busy life to distract myself from thoughts about my trauma.

The existence of more negative thoughts and feelings after the trauma is the third category. This one really hit home. The person may feel numb. They may forget about parts of the trauma or not be able to talk about it. They may think the world is not safe and can't trust anyone. They also may feel guilt or shame about the event, wishing they could have done something to prevent it. There can also be feelings of isolation and negative associations about oneself and the world. Category three was all about me.

The last category deals with excessive arousal, in which the person always feels on edge. The person may have difficulty concentrating, difficulty sleeping, be hypervigilant and irritable, startle easily, and have reckless behavior such as using drugs or alcohol. I had experienced all of these, except for reckless behavior.

There are also subtypes of PTSD. The type that pertains to me is PTSD with dissociation, in which the person feels disconnected from self and their surroundings.

This also can result in post-traumatic amnesia and difficulty interacting with others. I had trouble remembering events and new information for about thirty-five years after the explosion. I relied heavily on making schedules and to-do lists and keeping a daily journal. I also limited my socialization. I had a few friends, but I found it difficult to talk to new people, and I avoided being in a group of people.

Dr. Castronovo's diagnosis of PTSD was an eye-opener for me. I suddenly understood what had happened to me as a result of the bombing. My behavior was no longer a mystery to me, and it appeared that EMDR might be helpful. I was excited about my next session with Dr. Castronovo.

* * *

A week passed, and I was at my second session. We spent most of our time talking more about my symptoms, the process of EMDR, and what I could expect.

Dr. Castronovo told me, "You will have to explain the event in detail, which can be very painful and difficult. Do you think you are ready to do this? Do you think you *can* do this?"

"Yes," I responded.

I was willing to endure more emotional and physical pain in this process if it meant I could be free of the flashbacks, bodily pain, and overwhelming emotions that continued to haunt me. "How long will this take?" I inquired.

"It may take a couple of sessions to get through the treatment. I think you may go through the process sooner than many people because you have had so many years of therapy and seem ready and eager to get better."

"Yes, I want to get better. But how will it change my flashbacks and the pain?"

As he leaned back in his chair, he said, "When EMDR is complete, you should no longer be able to relive the bombing as if you were there. You won't be able to experience the pressure, smell the smoke, or visualize yourself in the Mobil office."

He paused for a minute and continued. "You'll still have the memory of the bombing, but the memory will no longer feel like present-tense reality. It will be like you are on a train, passing by the memory."

I visualized myself on a train, looking out the window.

"You can view the scene and describe it, but you will be on the outside," he said.

That would be amazing.

"So, what do you think? Are you still willing to try EMDR?"

I nodded my head.

"I think we can start next week. Let me explain the procedure to you and your homework for our next session."

This time, I was the one taking notes, not trusting my memory for homework.

Dr. Castronovo told me that I would describe a particular scene I remembered from the bombing. I would have to describe it out loud while tracking a series of lights on a bar in front of me. He mentioned that because I might feel increased anxiety during the procedure, he would be checking in with me to see how I was feeling and if I wanted to continue.

That sounded easy enough. Describe a scene while I watch flashing lights. Knowing that I could stop at any time if I became overwhelmed was comforting. Sounded safe to me.

"Your homework: You need to decide on the scene you want to focus on. You also should review the calming strategies you have learned from therapy to help you through any anxiety you may experience."

I scribbled down my homework and scheduled an appointment with Dr. Castronovo for the following week.

I drove the hour home, thinking how wonderful life could be without nightmares and flashbacks. I was hopeful that other physical reactions, the intense, overwhelming emotions. and my daily pain would cease. There were no guarantees, but I was willing to try. I wanted my life back.

The week between appointments went quickly. I decided to use diaphragmatic breathing exercises as my primary calming strategy. I selected a scene to describe.... the scene that always pops into my head the most and the one I find most disturbing....the scene where I find myself on the floor after the explosion. I was ready for my third session.

＊　＊　＊

My third session started with Dr. Castronovo reviewing the EMDR procedure. I made myself comfortable in the big reclining chair with lots of pillows as he showed me the light bar. It was a single bar mounted horizontally on a stand. There would be a series of lights on the bar, which I would follow with my eyes. He reminded me that when I was ready, I could start describing my scene while I followed the light with my eyes. I could stop at any time if I felt uncomfortable or experienced an emotional overload. I was ready to do this.

The light bar was in front of me as I started to visualize and describe the scene. My eyes started to follow the line of lights from left to right. I began my description.

"I am lying on my back on the floor of the employment office next to the gigantic potted plant. I'm staring at what is left of the ceiling. I see charred pieces of ceiling tile smoking and hanging in pieces."

I noted my breathing was becoming rapid and shallow, so I started to take long, deep breaths, watching my stomach expand upon inhalation.

"Check in with your feelings," said Dr. Castronovo. "You can stop if you need to. Keep watching the lights move across the board."

I continued despite feeling a little anxious.

"There is burning debris all around me, and the air is thick with smoke."

I let out a cough as I felt like smoke was filling my lungs. I cleared my throat and continued.

"Glass is everywhere, from the shattering of the plate glass window at the front of the office. I see blood on the walls and the floor."

"How are you feeling? You can stop at any time," he said.

I was now struggling with myself.

Part of me wanted to quit; the other part wanted to continue.

The smell of gunpowder is overpowering.

I can barely see through the thick smoke.

I'm watching pieces of the charred ceiling fall around me.

The giant philodendron is shielding me from debris. There's blood on the rug.

What has just happened? How did I get here?

The pressure on my chest and my head is unbearable. My head is about to explode.

"You can stop at any time," Dr. Castronovo interjected.

My eyes continued to focus on the flashing lights as I continued to describe the grizzly scene.

Left   Right

Left   Right

Left   Right

I blink my eyes several times as I realize that I am really in Dr. Castronovo's office. I make myself follow the blinking lights some more.

Left   Right

Left   Right

I felt like a rush of scalding steam was escaping from my scalp like a pressure cooker valve.

I held my breath and then let out a giant exhale.

I was no longer talking, but the lights were still moving across the board.

I started sobbing as I felt a weird sense of relief and calmness.

The pain had vanished.

I didn't realize how much negative stuff was stored in my body until it was gone.

I felt like a new person.

I felt like myself.

"It's over. I'm not broken anymore."

That was the end of my EMDR sessions.

I did have a few more meetings with Dr. Castronovo to follow up. He said that my rapid response to EMDR therapy was unusual—that most people required several sessions to process their trauma. He said that the many years of work that I did on myself in and outside of cognitive behavior therapy prepared me to be ready for the technique.

Even though I was technically ready for EMDR, it was not an easy process. It had to have been one of the most challenging things I have done. It was emotionally painful, and I relived my trauma in front of somebody. I felt so vulnerable but knew that I was safe during the process.

I felt like my nightmares, flashbacks, and lack—then, onslaught—of emotion had been validated by my work with Dr. Castronovo and that I was not crazy. I felt healed, especially after hearing some of his final words to me.

"You should write a book about this. It's such an interesting story."

I never considered my story interesting. It was just my life, and I wanted to find a way to live it without pain. The book idea appealed to me, and I would think seriously about it.

I never had another flashback or nightmare. I tried to relive the memories as a "test" but was unsuccessful. I could visualize the scene with the plant, but I felt nothing. There were no smells, no physical sensations, and no fears. The experience turned into an event that happened in the past that I was no longer an active part of. My ability to remember things from one day to the next returned. I never recovered the lost memories of moments in my life from August 3, 1977, up until my EMDR session in 2015, but I remember every day after. I had a lot to discover about myself, and this was one step closer. I opened my heart and mind to possibilities and experiences, determined to live my life to the fullest and create new memories. I would find myself again.

CHAPTER 13

ASHES AND SPARKS

After the EMDR session, I never relived that day in the Mobil employment office. However, in 2016, there seemed to be an increase in terrorism across the globe. All these acts of terrorism reminded me of my feelings, and I continued to empathize with the people involved in those attacks. I felt angry about terrorism, but I felt compassion for the victims and their families. The influx of emotion was both overwhelming and frightening for me. It wasn't my "stuff" to deal with, yet it felt like mine. I kept a journal about my PTSD symptoms and responses to these events.

March 22, 2016:

I heard about the bombing in Brussels on my way to work. Hearing this wants to disrupt my brain, but I won't let it. It's been almost thirty-nine years after the Mobil bombing, and the pain is still there. I thought I would be brave and watch the video of the bombing at the Brussels airport. I watched for five seconds and turned it off. I could feel pressure behind my eyes and pain in my head as I could see the smokey air. In fact, I could smell it, and it became hard to breathe. So many senses at once.

June 16, 2016:

I awoke this morning to the news of a mass shooting in Orlando, Florida: fifty dead and fifty-three wounded. A man walked into a gay bar during Pride Month and started shooting. The FBI and President Obama called it terrorism. So many people died and were physically and emotionally injured. I hurt inside for the survivors and their families. They will live a life of hell with memories of today and wondering why some people were killed and others were spared.

June 28, 2016:

Another terrorist attack in Turkey. There have been many this spring. Suicide bombers in the Turkey airport. Violent extremism. I can't be free of this.

July 3, 2016:

A bombing in a restaurant in India. ISIS takes responsibility, but India says ISIS is not there. Who knows, but almost forty dead. ENOUGH! It is hard to live with terrorism in the world. I don't get as preoccupied with it as I did in the past, but it is a persistent nag.

These events had a profound effect on me. They had nothing to do with my experience, yet I was filled with intrusive thoughts and questions about my existence and my recovery from trauma. Now that I was no longer reliving the bombing, I could think about terrorism in a more objective way rather than being triggered by every event. I understood the impact of terrorism on individuals, and I was able to empathize due to my own experience. I had a deep concern about other victims and their families, wondering how they would cope. I knew that the lives of these victims of terrorism and their loved ones were not my responsibility and that I could do nothing to help them, but somehow, I felt that I needed to.

Is this the reason I was spared? Am I supposed to provide support to other victims of violence? Help others? Change lives?

The idea was planted, but I had no idea how to make it a reality. I wanted to share my lessons learned:

Time does not heal all wounds.

PTSD responses become part of you.

PTSD responses can last a lifetime.

You can get better and move on with your life.

I wondered if writing a book would help me share these lessons.

My newly discovered empathy represented a change in my thinking and focus. I wasn't feeling quite so isolated and separate from the world anymore. I recognized that other people might be having emotional and physical reactions to their trauma that were similar to mine. I don't believe my emotions were "normal" when you consider the general population. I do believe that my feelings were typical for someone who experienced a severe trauma. Maybe a book would help other people get to where I am now.

*   *   *

Even though I felt like I had made a lot of progress, life was still challenging. Surprisingly, the hardest part of 2016 was not the increase in terrorism in the world or my responses to it. It was not my job or my dogs. It was the passing of my mother.

My mother was a positive thinker, took good care of herself, and was very creative. She always seemed to be grounded. The only thing I did not admire in her was her willingness to live in my father's shadow. He didn't want her to work, to have friends over if he was not around, and he would not allow her to disagree with him in public.

When he died, my mother blossomed. She started watercolor painting again. She entertained, traveled, and published a children's book and a short story. She thrived. She was a strong woman, and I think I inherited my strength and resilience from her.

My mom fell and broke her pelvis at the age of ninety-eight, after which she became progressively weak and confused. She could no longer live independently, so she moved to a supportive living environment, where she passed away on October 27, 2016. She was unhappy there, living with the "old people," as she said.

It's hard to lose a parent, especially if it is the second one and it is your mother. I felt like I lost a part of me when she died. She gave birth to me and raised me, and she influenced some of my personality traits, ideas, and accomplishments. I no longer had parents or grandparents. It made me realize that each of us is alone on this planet to discover who we are. I was sixty-one years old and still figuring that out.

My mother didn't want to have a funeral. Her wishes were to be cremated and have her ashes scattered in the ocean. My father wanted her to be buried next to him. My sister took care of all the arrangements and legal details, and I helped organize my mother's belongings.

My mother's ashes were put into three urns. One urn was to be buried in the cemetery next to my father. One was to be dropped into the ocean off the coast of Bermuda, her favorite place, and the third urn was to be dropped off the coast of Maine, where she lived for about thirty years.

Honestly, it never felt right for Mom to be divided into three parts. As an agnostic person, I am constantly questioning the origins and meaning of life, our purpose here on earth, and death. What is it like after you die? Are you in the same state of nothingness as you were before birth? Is it like sleep? I don't know if there is an afterlife or what that even means. I do believe people have souls, consisting of their emotions, inner being, and the pieces that made them who they are. The soul is a big piece—maybe even the center of your identity. Some people claim they communicate with the dead, and some people claim their loved ones who have passed on visit in their dreams or send them signs. I do know that my mom has appeared to me in dreams several times, and I have felt her presence. I keep her charm bracelet with the Dutch Dimes next to my bed. When I was around five years old, I asked my mother to leave me that bracelet when she died. That was bold of me, but she said she would. About fifty-five years later (a year before she died), she gave me that bracelet and said, "So we can stay connected." The bracelet stays on the bedside table, but sometimes, it moves to a different place. I've not been able to explain this other than its movement being representative of my mom telling me I need to think more about a decision or change my attitude.

So here's my question: After one dies, how important is the physical body (intact, embalmed or not, or cremated) to the existence of the soul? Was it OK that my mom's ashes were divided in three?

I continue to wonder.

* * *

We planned a trip to Bermuda for April 2017 and a boat trip in Maine in the summer months following.

Just before that Bermuda trip, probably around February 2017, I got another phone call from Bill, who had just returned to New Jersey after being in the Pacific for several months. I was so comfortable talking to him. Conversation was easy, and Bill talked a lot. We talked about work, my dogs, and people we were dating. While we were talking, I had a realization:

Bill has called me every time he comes home for the past ten years.

I didn't think a man would continue to call a woman who was "just a good person." I wanted to satisfy my curiosity about the possibility of this becoming a romantic relationship. After the EMDR, I felt like I had more control over my life and my triggers. I was feeling more emotionally available and wanted to be with another person. Even though I told myself I didn't want a long-distance relationship, I had to wonder if there was some romantic energy between us. I had closed the door on this possibility when we met in Boston in 2011, but now, in 2017, I was letting the door open.

"You know," I said coyishly. "Now that you're home, you could come up to visit me."

"I'd like that," he said. "Maybe I could stop by next time I visit my friends in Vermont. It's on the way,"

"No, take a better look at a map. Ashburnham is not on the way to Vermont," I responded quickly.

Then, the following words slipped out of my mouth like butter.

"Maybe you could just come up here for a weekend, like Memorial Day weekend?"

Surprised that I said that, I was appalled at the words I said next.

"I have a spare bedroom. In fact, I have a summer house you could stay in."

Silence.

I waited for Bill to reject the idea.

Then I heard, "Sure...I'll come up Memorial Day weekend."

"Ok, great!" I exclaimed, and we ended our phone conversation with a promise to make definite plans for Memorial Day weekend as the time got closer.

What just happened? I wasn't sure.

I now had two things to look forward to. A trip to Bermuda with my sister in a couple of months and a weekend with Bill the month after.

In the last week of April, my sister Karin and I flew to Bermuda for five days to release Mom into the ocean. My sister gave me the urn to pack. I decided to pack Mom in my suitcase, so I carefully wrapped up the urn, cushioning it with my clothes so it wouldn't break. I was a little worried about going through customs in Bermuda, but there were no problems.

After settling into the Fairmont Southampton, we set off to take one-third of Mom to her Bermuda resting place. I put the urn in my backpack, and we went on a long walk to explore the South Shore beaches to find the right place. I had no idea that the urn would be so heavy, and the load on my back seemed heavier with every step. I touched the teardrop ruby on my necklace as we walked along South Road to the beaches. I needed a little comfort on my way to say farewell to my mother.

After about an hour of walking, we found ourselves on an isolated beach with a thirty-foot cliff lined with coral. My sister thought that was the perfect place. Climbing the cliff and tossing the urn into the ocean was to be my job (so I found out). As my sister gave me explicit instructions on how/where to toss Mom, I realized it was impossible. There was a strong onshore wind that I had to fight to get up the hill. When I reached the top, I held the urn close to my heart and tightened the muscles in my legs to brace myself against the wind. I realized that when I tossed the urn, the ashes would blow back into me like a boomerang or I might lose my balance and fall off the cliff. I tried to convince my sister that this was not the best place, but she insisted.

I paused atop the coral cliff to send a few final thoughts to my mom.

Thanks for teaching me to be strong and independent.

I love you.

"Just throw it," Karin shouted with her hands cupped around her mouth.

So, I did. As I predicted, I tossed it straight out, and the wind took it towards the shore. It landed in a little sandy pool of ocean with crystal-clear turquoise water swirling above it. The tide was going out, and since the urn was bio-degradable, I knew it would dissolve, and Mom would be carried out to sea.

I climbed down the steep cliff, only to have my sister greet me with, "I think you need to go get that and do a better toss."

I had politely agreed to all my sister's suggestions, but not this time.

"You can get it if you think I didn't do a good enough job. I'm not climbing on any more coral and getting wet in the process."

My sister turned around and started walking up the beach towards the road. I knew her answer, so I followed her back to the road. My heart was heavy as I felt like I said a formal "goodbye" to my mother—at least one-third of her. I felt a little teardrop on my cheek.

On our way back to the hotel, Karin started reminiscing about things we did with Mom. The memories my sister spoke of were all after 1977, when we got together as adults. Karin loves to talk about the past, and I don't. Every sentence she spoke started with "Do you remember the time that...?" I remained quiet and listened with intrigue as it seemed to be new information to me.

How does she remember all of those times and details? I don't remember any of it.

We walked up the hill to the hotel, and she said, "Remember how much Mom liked your boyfriend, Paul? What ever happened to him?"

I stopped dead in my tracks. I turned to Karin and said, "I don't. In fact, I don't even remember anyone named Paul."

She looked me in the eye and said, "How could you forget that? We had such a good time with him and liked him so much!"

"I'm sorry. I just don't remember him at all. I don't remember any of the things you said."

And then she said what you should never say to someone with post-traumatic amnesia. "If you just try a little harder, I'm sure you'll remember."

That comment stabbed me in the hippocampus, the part of the brain responsible for memory formulation and storage. Although I knew that PTSD had robbed me of so many memories of life events, the fact that I couldn't remember experiences with my mother was devastating. I had to grieve not only for the loss of my mother but also for the loss of my memories of her.

The other tricky part about memory loss is the connection to your identity. Our past experiences and memories of them create the person we become. If you can't recall your past, you feel like you are floating around, trying to figure out who you are. Photographs verified events in my past, such as family gatherings and weddings, but I did not truly remember them. At age sixty-two, I still did not feel connected to anyone or anything.

After my sister's comment, I realized that she didn't understand or recognize that I didn't remember much after the bombing. Even though I am sure I told her, she just didn't get it. I reached up to touch my ruby teardrop necklace to give me comfort and composure.

My fingers touched my bare neck where the ruby teardrop usually rested. There was nothing there.

Maybe my necklace is twisted and is higher up on my neck.

My fingers frantically walked up and behind my neck.

Maybe the clasp broke, and it is in my bra.

I stuck my hand down my blouse and did a thorough sweep of my bra, searching for the chain with the small diamond and ruby teardrop.

It's gone. My necklace is gone.

"My necklace!" I exclaimed. "My necklace is gone,"

It was my talisman that protected me.

"I've worn it for over forty years."

A sense of panic came over me.

It was the one thing that connected my past to my present.

I was devastated. I relied on that necklace to remind me I survived, that I was present, that I was safe.

"We'll go to Hamilton tomorrow, and you can buy a new one," said Karin, not aware of the significance of the loss.

Nothing would ever replace my necklace with the diamond chip and ruby teardrop, but maybe wearing something else around my neck would make me feel better.

The next day, we went into Hamilton, and I bought myself a gold necklace with a bar containing six small diamonds in a row. My "safety" necklace was gone, but I bought something different. This one commemorated my mother, her strength, independence, and ability to make the best of whatever life presented to her. Maybe the loss of my teardrop necklace was Mom's way of telling me that I didn't need her or a necklace to give me strength—that the power and resilience to find myself, protect myself, and live the life I wanted was within me.

* * *

It was the beginning of May when we got home from Bermuda. Karin returned to Maine, where she lived, and I returned to Massachusetts. It wasn't long before I got a phone call from Bill to confirm our plans to meet over Memorial Day. I was excited and did not regret extending the invitation to him to visit me. With so many things to think about, I was glad I had a couple of weeks to mentally prepare myself for his visit. I considered the weekend a test.

The test questions were:

Is there a mutual spark between us?
If yes, do I want to pursue a relationship with Bill?

And the deal breaker questions:

Will he like the dogs, and will Turner give his approval?

I knew that if the answer was "no" to any of the questions, then we would move on as friends because we are both, in his words, "good people."

Bill drove up on a Friday afternoon, and the original plan was for him to leave on Sunday morning. I got the spare bedroom and my summer cottage a few miles away ready for a guest so he could choose where he wanted to stay. On Friday, we talked well into the evening and then decided to go for a walk. We strolled down the dark dirt road by my house. The moon was a sliver in its waxing crescent phase, so the only illumination was from the brilliant stars above us. The sound of the tree frogs was the background music as we walked in silence, holding hands. I felt the sparks of romance.

Needless to say, Bill did not sleep in the spare house or bedroom for the next two nights.

Sunday morning came, and we enjoyed a quick breakfast in my kitchen as we said our goodbyes. He put his duffle bag in his car and returned for a final goodbye that lasted until seven that evening.

"I've really got to go now," he said quietly. "It's Sunday night, and it may take five hours to get home."

He got up, walked to the door, and stood there, looking at me. I felt really awkward. I wanted to get up, but I wanted to keep my distance. I had the same feeling as our Boston farewell. I decided to act on my emotions, went over to him, and kissed him on the cheek.

I needed to confirm that the answer to my three questions was "yes." He seemed to get along well with the dogs, especially Alden, who spent time on his lap. Turner did not get between us and was more interested in his toys than Bill, so that was a good sign. Now, to confirm Bill's feelings.

I wanted to trust my intuition—after all, he had shared my bed with me. But I didn't think that was enough to confirm. What if it had just been a two-time thing?

I had been wrong in the past due to my poor insight and inability to interpret all the nonverbal signals. I didn't trust my interpretation of the very obvious signals that Bill was attracted to me. I wanted verbal confirmation, so I was going to ask.

"Thanks for coming up. I had a great time," I said, realizing those weren't the words I wanted to say.

"I had a good time too. Glad I made the trip," Bill confirmed.

My heart was beating faster as I squeezed out my next sentence.

"Where do we want to go with this? Friends? More than friends?"

I held my breath a little as I waited for Bill's response.

"I think we should see where this takes us," he said.

And with that, he gave me a quick hug, turned, and walked out the door to his car.

As he drove away, a few tears trickled down my cheeks. I realized that this was an "old" response—a pre-bombing response. My teary response to Bill leaving made me feel "normal" since this used to happen when I said important goodbyes—leaving Bermuda, leaving close friends and family that I didn't see very often.

I looked forward to seeing him again to "see where this takes us."

Bill came to visit me again two weeks later, just before he went back to sea. This time, he would sail near Singapore, so it would be six months or more before we saw each other. He promised to call and kept his promise. In fact, we did a Zoom call every night he was away.

The summer weather of 2017 was upon us in New England, and my sister told me that she had made arrangements to have my mother's ashes spread off the Coast of Port Clyde, Maine, where my parents had lived for about thirty years. Due to Maine regulations, we had to hire a boat to take us three miles from the shore. Again, holding and tossing the urn was my job, which was much easier to do from the boat than from the top of a cliff.

It was a sunny, warm day with a light breeze. I said my final farewell to Mom as I tossed the urn overboard. I had a bouquet of Maine wildflowers with me, and I dropped one flower at a time into the ocean. The flowers swayed back and forth in the wake of the boat, leaving a lovely trail of color to commemorate my mother.

When the boat docked in Port Clyde, Karin and I walked through the town and by my mother's house for the last time. The house was sold in April, and we no longer had access to it, but I needed to say one last goodbye to the house. After walking around the property, we got in my sister's car and drove ninety minutes back to her home in Phippsburg, Maine.

"I finally opened some of the boxes Mom had packed away," she said as she drove down Route 1.

"Did you find anything interesting?" I asked as I gazed out the car window at the coastal scenery.

"There are some boxes of photographs we can go through. Photos of Dad, our grandparents, and photos of us as kids."

"Anything else of interest?"

"There's a lot of memorabilia from Bermuda that you can have."

"Well, I already have a lot of Bermuda things I saved from when we lived there, but I'll take it."

We finished the drive, admiring the scenery along the way, anticipating the excitement and drudgery of unboxing what my mother had saved.

We walked into my sister's house, sat in the kitchen, and had coffee. I could see several piles of boxes from my mom's house on the living room floor.

"How should we start to go through these boxes?" I asked.

"I've already opened them. Let's empty them and make piles of things to keep and things to toss."

We got up from the kitchen table and sat on the living room floor, surrounded by musty-smelling boxes. The cardboard was not crisp and firm but soft and bendable from sitting in a dark, damp closet for years.

The first box I sorted through had a variety of musty-smelling books about Bermuda, old recipes written in my mom's sloppy penmanship where *n*'s looked like *r*'s, and tattered newspaper articles about all of our accomplishments in school, sports, and music when we were kids. My mother was a great saver of everything related to us kids, from our kindergarten report cards to our high school graduation programs.

I made a pile of things I wanted—old photos, my baby book, and Bermuda memorabilia from the early '70s when we lived there. I added my tattered, yellow first-grade report card to the pile. I had to keep this fifty-seven-year-old document because of the comment that Miss Goltz, the teacher, made about me: "TALKS TOO MUCH."

I was really enjoying finding things from my pre-bombing years when Karin handed me a tan envelope.

"Here's something you might be interested in," she said.

In her hand was an eight-by-twelve envelope with the words *Mobil bombing* printed in my mom's handwriting.

As I took the envelope from her, she added, "I took a look inside, and there are news reports, magazine articles, and photographs related to the Mobil bombing."

It's like my sister handed me a bundle of trauma neatly concealed in an envelope. I didn't want to touch it, fearing that some contents would leap into my fingers and trigger me. Reading about the past might invite it back into my present, and I was not ready to look at it.

For lack of anything else to say, I said "Thanks" and tucked the envelope in my overnight bag. When I returned home, I slotted it neatly in the back of my filing cabinet, which stayed unopened for almost a year.

CHAPTER 14

TWISTS AND TURNS

The remainder of 2017 played out on a happier note. Work was going well. I altered my work commitments so that I had my private practice part-time, but I also worked in a high school to provide more consistent income, working fewer hours to give me more time to work with my dogs. In December, Bill and I spent a week in Orlando, Florida, with one of my Boston Terriers, Buzz, who had qualified for the North American Diving Dogs National Championship at the Orange County Convention Center in Orlando. It was a fun week, culminating with Buzz winning sixth place in the Novice Division for Distance jumping.

After that week, it was evident that our relationship was evolving into something very special. As far as I was concerned, any man who could spend a week with me at a dog competition was a keeper.

"I'd like to take you out for dinner for your birthday in August," he said with a twinkle in his eye.

"That sounds great," I responded, wondering why he wanted to make plans for my birthday, which was nine months away,

"Think of a special place you'd like to go to for dinner," he said.

"Well, I will think it over, but there are many great places to eat in Worcester or even Boston," I answered.

Laughing, he added, "Those aren't special places. I was thinking more like London, Venice, or Paris."

I was dumbfounded. "That's a huge invitation, and thank you. But I can't afford a trip like that right now—just for dinner."

"Think about it," he said in a thoughtful tone. "I'll cover the airfare and hotel. You pick the place, the hotel, and the restaurant, and I'll take care of everything else."

He can't be serious about this. What's the catch?

But he was sincere, and there was no catch.

At the end of January 2018, I chose Paris for my birthday, and we began planning our trip, which was so exciting but also anxiety-provoking. Shortly after I agreed to the trip, I realized that we were going during the timespan of my anniversary reaction, when I might become highly anxious, depressed, and dissociate. I wasn't sure I would be up to traveling in August, especially to France, where there had been a terrorist attack in the Paris Orly Airport the previous year. We were going through the Charles de Gaulle Airport, which is bigger and more crowded, and I wondered what the odds were for a terrorist attack in that airport.

A month passed since we had started planning for Paris, and I wanted to explain my past and my concerns to Bill. I felt a little guilty because I probably should have shared it all sooner. It was a hard conversation for me to have because I would have to reveal my PTSD, and I was worried he might reject me. I needed to tell him before we confirmed our flights and hotel reservation in case he changed his mind about going with me.

One afternoon, we played with the dogs in my living room in Ashburnham. Nadia chewed a bone on the couch, Turner was involved with a squeaky toy, and Alden raided the toy box when I said, "We need to talk about our Paris trip."

"Okay," Bill replied as he tossed the stuffed birthday cake toy for Alden, which he continued to do for another five minutes. "Is it about the hotel? Did you pick a restaurant for your birthday dinner?"

"No, it's not that."

I described the events of August 3, 1977, to Bill. Turner sat close by me, allowing my hands to execute long, deep strokes down his back. He put his head on my lap, and I scratched his ears.

Bill listened attentively and stopped throwing the birthday cake for Alden. Alden was still plopping the cake toy onto Bill's lap, but Bill was focused on my story.

"That's horrible," he said. "I'm sorry that happened to you."

I was amazed that he reacted without judgment and without dismissing my emotions and concerns.

I could see Bill had a puzzled look on his face.

Bill's expression changed to concern.

"What are you worried about?"

"I'm worried about a terrorist attack in the airport."

I thought the answer was obvious and wondered if Bill thought I was being ridiculous.

"There have been more terrorist attacks all over the world, and there was recently an attack in the other Paris airport, Orly. I'm worried about being in another attack."

I am not sure he understands how difficult going through the airport will be for me.

I waited for his response.

"I doubt that is likely to happen. There's increased security in all the airports these days," he said.

I let out a big sigh.

"That's true, but it doesn't make my anxiety go away."

"You can't live your life in fear. You shouldn't isolate yourself because of what you think might happen," he said as he tossed Alden's cake into the next room.

He has a good point. That's a practical response.

"Anyway," he continued, "In my line of work, I've been trained to act in situations with violence. You never know what might happen when you are in certain places in this world at sea. You'll be safer with me. I promise."

Bill isn't going to be able to prevent a terrorist attack, but I think he is going to be able to think fast and act if there is any threat or real violence.

"I think you're right about not isolating myself because of my thoughts about what might happen." I added, "But I can't turn off my anxiety. You need to know that."

"I understand," he assured me.

I continued talking about my PTSD symptoms, my previous therapy, and EMDR. I explained that EMDR was most helpful in eliminating my flashbacks but that I still experienced anxiety, fear, and concern regarding any acts of violence.

Turner got up and walked over to his bed. Alden found another toy to bring to Bill, and Nadia remained on the couch, chewing her bone.

I felt relieved now that Bill and I discussed the Mobil bombing and my fears. Maybe my fears were unrealistic, but they were real to me. I was happy that Bill understood and accepted my feelings and concerns. He didn't reject me as I had feared. His response seemed both logical and supportive.

I can get through the airport with this man.

I'm really looking forward to my Paris trip, but I just wish all the threats of violence would stop in the world.

Despite my wish for violence to stop, it was on the rise. In the first twenty-one weeks of 2018, there were twenty-three school shootings where someone was hurt or killed. These school shootings bothered me—the motivation for the violence was different from terrorism, but it was violence just the same. News reports of school violence were having a profound effect on my ability to concentrate and work effectively with my students, some of whom were terrified that a shooter would show up on campus.

On Wednesday, February 14, 2018, in Parkland, Florida, a gunman, a former student who was expelled, went to Marjory Stoneman Douglas High School and killed seventeen people in six and a half minutes. I listened to an abbreviated news report that night, used my strategies to manage my anxiety, and was prepared for my own work at school the following day. I wondered how the students and the school administration would react to the events in Parkland. Although Parkland was almost fifteen hundred miles away, I knew students would worry about their safety in our school community. Social media already put me in a place of heightened anxiety, and I wondered how it would affect the students in the high school where I worked.

How will my students react to this tomorrow? I will need to make them feel safe so they can focus on their work. What can I say to them to make them feel secure when I don't feel safe?

Thursday morning, there was minimal discussion about Parkland. In fact, the school administrators advised the faculty not to bring up the topic with students. After I finished my morning speech therapy sessions, I sat at my desk to read my emails. There was one from the high school principal that grabbed my attention:

TO: All High School Faculty

This is to inform you that there has been a threat of violence against our high school. The situation has been evaluated by the local police department and Homeland Security. It has been determined that this is just a threat and does not jeopardize the safety of our students and staff.

We will remain in school given these findings. A letter of explanation will be sent home to parents from the superintendent this afternoon. Please do not discuss this with your students as you do not have all the details, and the threat is still under investigation.

My thoughts brought me back to the day of the Mobil bombing when we were told that we were "safe" because the NYPD Bomb Squad checked the building. My stomach churned, and I felt like choking on the unpleasant feeling in my throat.

I don't feel like the school administrators are taking this seriously.

As I listened to the news later that day, I learned there had been an uptick in threats of school violence all over the country after the news reports about Parkland. I didn't sleep well that night. I felt less safe than usual.

That Friday at school was difficult for me. There were discussions among students and staff about our safety and more follow-up by the police department. Apparently, the community was in an uproar over the threats of violence, and the investigations continued. Yet, staff and students were to proceed as usual. More intrusive thoughts about the August 3, 1977, events filled my head. I would not allow myself to be put into that situation again.

I made it through the day without a panic attack, but by the time the school day was over, I was exhausted, couldn't concentrate, and felt helpless in a situation that I could not control.

I need to go home where I can feel safe.

Once home, I immediately went to bed and slept until noon Saturday. I felt like crap and couldn't motivate myself to do anything.

On Saturday, I stayed in my pajamas and spent most of my time sitting in the kitchen chair, staring out the window.

I am going to cancel my plans to go out with friends tonight.

I stayed home. I could barely care for the dogs; only their need for my care got me out of the kitchen chair.

I then went back into my disassociated state.

At some point, I fell asleep back in that chair.

I woke up early Sunday with my head on the kitchen table. I felt alert but exhausted. My neck hurt from sleeping awkwardly, and I hadn't showered since Thursday night. I made myself some cinnamon toast and a steaming cup of double espresso, giving me the jump start I needed to escape from the kitchen table.

I walked upstairs into the bathroom and turned the shower faucet handle to the right to hot. I peeled off the clothes I had been wearing since Friday morning and stepped into a haze of steam. The condensation encapsulated my body, making me feel warm and safe. As the beads of water rhythmically tapped on my back, I contemplated my reaction to the threat of violence at school.

I don't know how to handle this. Maybe I need more EMDR.

Although EMDR prevented me from reliving the day of the bombing, I could still experience disassociation from the threat of another violent attack.

I turned the shower knob to the left, turning off the spray, and just enjoyed the vigor of the hazy steam left in the shower stall for a few moments. I stepped out of the shower and put on my warm-up pants and sweatshirt. I played fetch and tug with the dogs for a while, which released some energy and tension for all of us. When the dogs decided they had had enough, Nadia and Alden jumped on the couch. Turner sat by my side, leaning into me and gently putting his head on my lap to be petted.

I grabbed my journal and started writing my thoughts about the Parkland shooting and the threats in the high school where I worked. Journaling still helped me organize my feelings and get intrusive thoughts out of my head.

After a couple of hours of writing, I made myself a bowl of pasta with butter and went to bed. Although I slept soundly on Saturday and Sunday nights, I awoke to brain fog and lethargy on Monday morning. The piercing sound of my alarm and the presence of Turner throwing his toys on my chest prompted me to get out of bed. The dogs were hungry; my four-legged family needed to be fed. I dragged myself down the stairs and let them out into the dog run for their morning constitutional.

While they were outside, I prepared their breakfast. What was typically an automatic task required concentration and checking to make sure I was giving the correct supplements and amount of food to each dog as I struggled to organize the simple task of breakfast prep for three dogs. I realized I was in no condition to work with students. I took a sick day.

Around noon on Monday, I called Dr. Castronovo and made an appointment for the following week to discuss having more EMDR. I felt like I lost control of myself over the weekend, and I didn't have the tools to prevent the disassociation from happening again. I realized that the EMDR did not cure me or eliminate the possibility of a reaction to other stimuli associated with any threat of violence.

Tuesday morning, I was back at school. I turned on my computer and read an email from the principal with the subject line "Update." So, I opened it.

My jaw dropped, and my stomach went sour as I read that the local police were continuing their investigation of the threats from last week. We were also notified that we would be required to attend training on how to respond to school shootings.

WHAT? Five days later, the police are still investigating? I don't think we are really safe.

I could feel myself getting hotter and hotter with anger and anxiety. I realized that the way this was being handled was impacting my mental health and my ability to work. I made an appointment to speak with the principal later that morning.

The principal was a tall man in his forties. He was well-liked by the students and staff for his ability to listen to concerns. However, he was a marshmallow when standing up for staff and students when a situation got heated. I always thought his actions were limited by the administrators in the main office of the entire school district because he seldom followed up his supportive words with actions.

He was not an independent thinker. He was like the parent who said they were your friend but enforced new rules without telling you. If you broke them, you got sent to your room without supper.

"Good morning, sir," I said as I entered his stuffy office. "I need to talk to you about the threats of violence and how they are affecting me."

"Have a seat," he said, gesturing to the chair directly across from his giant mahogany desk. "Everyone is concerned, and everyone is upset."

"My situation may be different," I said with my voice wavering. "In 1977, I worked in New York City, and my office was bombed. There was a threat and a police investigation, but we were never told there was a threat."

I paused to take a few deep breaths.

"We were not safe, and a bomb went off ten feet from my desk. I was lucky to survive. Any threats of violence at work are hard for me to deal with because I never feel safe."

He looked at me blankly, "Oh," he said. "What else?"

I could not believe he did not acknowledge the severity of my trauma and my fear of any lack of safety.

"I was wondering if you could change the subject line of your emails to something other than 'Update' and indicate that they are about school safety. Reading about threats of violence during my school day sets off my anxiety and may elicit a panic attack."

I sat up taller in my chair to collect myself and continue.

"I'd like advance notice of lockdown drills."

He nodded his head as if in agreement.

He seems to understand and may agree with my requests.

"I heard we are going to have active shooter training. I'd like to get the training individually and in a format without videos or pictures. Those are triggering for me."

I let out a big sigh of relief from being able to share my story and advocate for myself.

"What do you want from me?" he barked. "I can't send you a separate email or go to you in person every time there is a threat. It's too much trouble to change the title of emails just for you."

Silence.

He added, "I can't give you special treatment."

I stood up, with tears rolling down my cheeks. "You have no idea....what this is doing to me," I sobbed.

He turned his eyes downward to his desk, avoiding eye contact.

"You need to be informed for your and everyone else's safety."

I turned around to leave his office and get my lesson ready for my next speech therapy student. I questioned whether I could continue working in this environment—an environment that was not supportive of the faculty and was toxic.

A week passed, and I had my appointment with Dr. Castronovo. I explained the events that transpired at my job at school and my reaction in the days following.

"I had a really bad reaction to a threat of a violent attack at school," I said, followed by describing all the details of that weekend I sat in the kitchen chair.

"Do you think I need more EMDR?"

"EMDR is good for processing memories of specific traumatic events," Dr. Castronovo explained, "But it won't stop you from having reactions to other triggers, such as the threat of violence."

My heart sank as I thought that there was no hope to eliminate my responses to triggers.

"Something that can help you is acceptance and commitment therapy," he added.

"Tell me more."

"This therapy teaches you to accept your negative and/or intrusive thoughts and focus on positive changes. You have the power and freedom to choose your actions and responses to a situation."

I have the power and the freedom to choose my actions and responses.

That resonated with me.

"I'd like to try this," I said optimistically. "I want to be able to control my responses."

We worked on changing my response patterns. After a few months, I had the tools to recognize that thoughts could not hurt me and that I had the power to change my thoughts. It sounds so simple, but it was not an easy change. This way of thinking is powerful and effective, but it is a continuous, fluid process. I had to remind myself to think this way so I didn't get caught in negative or destructive thoughts. Although I was learning to control my thoughts, sometimes they still got the best of me, and I would get stuck in old response patterns and have panic attacks.

✶ ✶ ✶

Sometime in March of the same year, the high school faculty and staff were required to attend a training on handling school shooters. I checked with the principal, and my previous request to be excused from this group training was not honored. I was told it was mandatory, and I was not to be given "special treatment."

It was a Thursday afternoon after the students went home. About forty faculty and staff gathered in the lecture hall to attend active shooter training provided by the local police. We were all seated on metal chairs in rows with a large television monitor at the front of the room. The training started with a video of the 1999 Columbine school shooting to heighten staff awareness of the seriousness of school violence. Everyone in the room was silent as the video began.

The opening scene was a man entering a school holding a rifle, knocking on doors, and preparing to shoot up the school. I watched for about a minute before my head felt like exploding. I felt the need to run.

I stood up before realizing I was doing it and ran out of the room. I was self-evacuating from a triggering situation.

Seconds later, I found myself walking down the long hallway to the main lobby.

As I faced the stairwell to the second floor, I was compelled to climb up the two flights of stairs. Step by step, I climbed to the top, where I stopped for a second. After the brief hesitation, my body turned right into the long corridor with empty classrooms on either side. I started walking and picked up the pace as I walked the length of the building to another stairwell.

Out of breath, I ran down two flights of stairs, skipping steps as I went.

At the bottom, I briskly walked through the cafeteria and back to the main lobby. I turned left and went up the stairwell again to the second floor.

I couldn't catch my breath.

My heart was racing.

I was on a mission to go somewhere, but I didn't know where.

I repeated this sequence of navigating the stairs and the hallways four more times. It seemed to be a meaningless action until, on my fifth trip through the cafeteria, it dawned on me that I was re-enacting the evacuation from the Mobil building.

It's not real. It's a thought. I am making myself do this, and I can make myself stop.

I slowed myself down, taking one step at a time, allowing me to utilize the concept I was learning in therapy. *I have the ability to change my behavior.*

One step at a time, I went through the cafeteria doors, into the lobby, and into the hallway by the lecture room. Now standing by the lecture room door, I stopped.

When I opened the door, it squeaked enough for some people to turn around and look at me. Feeling self-conscious, I went back inside, acting like nothing had happened. I sat down and pretended I was paying attention to the officer's lecture. I heard none of it. I was focused on my breathing and trying not to call any attention to myself.

I was recovering from a panic attack.

When the training was over, I went home and went to bed. I always feel better after I nap after a panic attack. I stayed home the next day due to the emergence of a migraine, which often appeared after a panic attack.

This all would have been avoidable if only I had been warned about the graphic displays of violence and allowed to receive the training in another format. No one from the school approached me about my exit from the lecture room. Nobody seemed to notice, or they were afraid to ask.

It was obvious that the school administrators didn't understand PTSD and silent mental health issues even though they had just provided a workshop to teachers on dealing with students who have sustained trauma. Teacher training involved developing sensitivity to students who have had a traumatic past and providing accommodations so that they could be more effective learners. The same principles obviously didn't apply to teachers and staff.

In therapy, I discussed with Dr. Castronovo how the school administrators had treated me, and I decided to file for accommodations through the Americans with Disabilities Act. The process was to write a letter to the HR department to request accommodations in the workplace that I felt I needed to be productive and manage my anxiety. I asked for several modifications to circumvent my triggers. These included receiving advanced notice of scheduled active shooter drills, lock-down drills, or evacuation drills; allowing me to take ten- to fifteen-minute breaks if needed to implement strategies to cope with anxiety/stress; excusing me from group trainings regarding the management of workplace violence but providing training to me individually without showing videos or photographs; allowing my service dog, Turner, to accompany me to work; that I not be given primary responsibility to organize or implement disaster or evacuation procedures for students; and providing sensitivity training to coworkers and supervisors about PTSD.

All of my requests were denied except for one: They agreed to allow me to take fifteen-minute breaks as long as they didn't interfere with my student therapy schedule or meeting attendance. That, in essence, was a denial.

I felt defeated, unsupported, and angry. I was furious that a school district that required teaching training on dealing with students' trauma did not or would not deal with staff's trauma. The district administrators commented that I should no longer be affected by the Mobil bombing since it happened so long ago. This made me think the administration thought I was overly dramatic for attention. I contemplated appealing the administration's decision by taking my requests to the teachers' union. The union's attorney informed me that the process would be lengthy, expensive, and traumatizing and probably would not change anything. Part of me felt that I should fight back because there needed to be a heightened awareness of silent emotional disabilities. However, the other part of me did not have the emotional stamina to fight. Either way, I was going to be riddled with guilt. I decided that I needed to do what was best for my mental health.

My resignation was effective at the end of June.

The loss of this contract job was very unsettling. I still had other contracts and clients in my private practice, but this loss represented half of my income. Ending a contract without another lined up to replace it was worrisome. In the long run, it was the best move for my mental health, but in the short term, I wasn't going to be able to pay my bills.

I immediately started looking for per diem or part-time work to generate enough income and fit in with my other scheduled contracts. I spent the month of July and the beginning of August doing job interviews. My résumé was full of experience, and I could work in almost any setting. The problem I had was in the interview. I had always gotten my previous jobs through word of mouth, and they were all offered to me without an interview. I had always been sought after. This was the first time since my early career that I was in the position of job seeker.

In several interviews, I found myself sitting at a table with three or more people, all firing questions about my philosophy of treatment and work experience. To my surprise, the stress of the situation would make my mind go blank. Part of an interview might have gone like this:

Interviewer: "How would you handle a parent angry about their child's lack of progress in therapy?"

Me: "I would schedule a meeting with them to discuss their concerns."

Interviewer: "Is that all? Anything else you would do?"

Me: "That would be my first step. I mean, it's hard to be more specific than that without knowing the child and why the parent is angry."

Interviewer: "Are you sure about that?"

Silence.

Are you sure? Are you sure? Anything else? Are you sure?

My mind went blank as it did with the same questions the FBI and NYPD posed many years ago.

I would lose my train of thought, and the interview would fall apart. I left with the promise that they'd get back to me, but they never did. I was a qualified speech-language pathologist, but when my responses were questioned, I lost all confidence and couldn't speak. This happened during four interviews in July.

On August 1, I received an email about a job opening that seemed perfect. It was a two-day-per-week position working with middle school students on social communication skills. I quickly filled out an application, and I received this email response:

"We received your application. Can you come in for an interview on August 8, 2018, at 1:00 p.m.?"

My heart skipped a beat when I got the interview, but I would be in Paris on August 8.

I responded:

"I would love to come in for an interview. Unfortunately, I am leaving for Paris on August 7 and will be returning on August 17. Can we reschedule for a different time?"

By the end of the day, I received this message:

Can you come in this Friday, August 3, at 10:00 a.m.?

I did not realize that the interview date was the same as the anniversary of the Mobil bombing. I confirmed the appointment, and I had my interview two days later. Two people were interviewing me. They asked me straightforward questions about my philosophy and work experience. They did not once question the accuracy of my responses with "Are you sure?" or "Is that all?" As a result, I had no memory lapses and could stay focused during our interaction. I was offered the job on the spot, and my work would begin the week after I returned from Paris. I was proud and relieved that I had a successful interview. I should have been even more proud that I did not have an anniversary reaction that year and managed an interview on the anniversary date.

Bill and I made it to Paris on August 8 and spent a thrilling ten days going to museums, averaging over twenty thousand steps per day, walking through the city, sightseeing, and eating. Unlike previous years, my anniversary reactions were much lower in frequency and intensity. The excitement of the trip and being with Bill overpowered my usual August sense of doom and gloom. I managed to get through the Charles de Gaulle Airport by leaving all the navigation and decision-making to Bill. I needed to conserve my mental energy for my relaxation strategies instead of figuring out how to get through the airport and then to the hotel. I have found this to be a very useful strategy to this day. Giving control to others I trust allows me to focus on managing my emotions and reactions. Works. Every. Time.

On my birthday, we went to the Eiffel Tower. There were so many people, and we waited in line for an hour to get to the stairs. We climbed almost seven hundred steps to the second level and then took the lift to get to the top. We were elbow to elbow with strangers in the tiny lift. For my petite stature, it was nose to armpit, and I couldn't wait to get off. We finally made it to the top observation deck. In five minutes, I felt dizzy and out of breath. The pressure inside my head was building, and the intrusive thoughts had started.

There are too many people up here.

What if we have to evacuate?

The thought of moving all these people on the lifts and the stairwell was frightening. What if the lifts no longer work? I had heard the stairs from the second floor to the top were closed to the public. Could they be used for evacuation? Would people be stuck on the top?

I became fixated on what would happen if a bomb went off somewhere on the Eiffel Tower. I could tell Bill how I was feeling, and we left. I don't think he enjoyed the crowds with screaming toddlers in strollers and was happy to leave sooner, too.

That night, we had an amazing dinner for my birthday. I will never forget the parmesan ice cream with caramelized onions we ate at a five-star restaurant. The rest of the trip was great, and I became addicted to Nespresso and croissants every morning. It was a wonderful time.

A couple of my friends placed bets as to whether I would receive a marriage proposal on the trip. There was no marriage proposal, but we did start to talk about the possibility of marriage in the future. Bill accepted me for who I was. He did not minimize my past, nor did he dramatize it. Bill saw me as a whole person and loved me for being me.

When I asked him why he loved me, he would tell me it was because I was smart, witty, sarcastic, energetic, independent, and attractive. I had not identified with those adjectives, but realizing that this was his perception of me created a sensation of near normalcy. I still had feelings of self-doubt, anxiety, and insecurity, but maybe a new identity was blossoming. Bill was helping me see my identity unfold.

CHAPTER 15

PANDORA'S BOX

The trip to Paris, leaving my job, and finding a new one made for a very stressful first part of 2018. But another major stressor that spring was cleaning out my filing cabinet. One day, I was busy in my office reviewing and throwing out old paperwork, as I did every spring. Throwing out papers was a feel-good activity for me, but not today. As I pulled the second drawer out, there, in the back, was the envelope labeled "Mobil bombing." I had forgotten about that envelope that I tucked away almost a year ago—my mother's collection of my trauma, my Pandora's Box.

If I open it, I'm faced with all the evil and trauma from my past. If I open it, I'm releasing my trauma into the world. If I open it, I will let my past seep into my present.

Then, I recalled another part of the Pandora fable.

Or, perhaps, like the box Zeus gave to Pandora, it contains the spirit of hope. If I open it, maybe I will find missing pieces about my past that will give me hope for the future. Maybe you have to let the negative stuff out to let hope in. Maybe there is hope for understanding my past and who I am today.

My curiosity and desire for hope got the best of me, and in that moment, like Pandora, I opened the envelope and pulled out the contents. In my hands were several newspaper and magazine articles about the Mobil bombing and the FALN.

I placed the forty-year-old, tattered, yellow articles on the table before me and read them. One by one, I read each article. My eyes raced across the faded print as my heart thumped into my throat. Reading the words about the bombing validated my responses to the terror I had experienced. It also confirmed the effectiveness of EMDR. I thought for sure that the articles would trigger me into reliving the attack, but instead, I was an outside observer, reading about a horrific series of events. When I was finished reading, I put the articles in a new folder, which remained on my desk.

I read those articles over and over again. It was a dose of reality that I could finally think about and absorb. With each read, the content became less painful. I learned new information about the day of the bombing and the trial, but there were still things I did not understand.

I wondered, again, if I should write a book as Dr. Castronovo had suggested in one of my early EMDR sessions. I started considering possibly writing a nonfiction book, but I needed more historical information and facts.

I didn't understand much about the FALN and the people involved. I needed to understand more about terrorism and the FALN if I was going to write a book about it. I jotted down a few of my questions:

What was the mission of the FALN?

What happened to Marie Torres after the federal trial?

What happened to other people affected by the Mobil bombing?

I started researching terrorism and the FALN. I ordered books, and I searched the internet. There was no internet in the 1970s and 1980s, but in 2018, there was plenty of information available on the internet about terrorism, specifically domestic terrorism. I found more newspaper articles, the transcription of the federal trial, and photographs. I even found an article in the *New York Daily News* dated January 18, 2017, that contained an interview with Steven Steinberg, the brother of Charles Steinberg, who was killed in the Mobil bombing. The article talked about Steven's outrage at the politically motivated prison releases of FALN members, specifically Oscar López Rivera, by Presidents Clinton and Obama.

The FALN was thought to be responsible for at least 130 bombings, and it was designated a terrorist organization. Most of the FALN members who were found guilty of their involvement with terrorism were sentenced to fifty or more years in prison. In 1999, President Clinton offered commutation of prison sentences for sixteen FALN members with the condition that they would refrain from any further violence. They had been convicted of crimes such as seditious conspiracy, possession of unregistered firearms, and interstate transportation of a stolen vehicle. They were found guilty of participating in the planning and execution of many bombings, including Fraunces Tavern in 1975 and the Mobil bombing in 1977.

There were reports that President Clinton thought the sentences were disproportionate to the crimes. Some people believed that the Clinton clemency was politically motivated to get the Puerto Rican vote for his wife Hillary, who was running for an open Senate seat in New York.

Then, in 2017, President Obama granted clemency to Oscar López Rivera, one of the primary leaders of the FALN. This man was considered to be one of the most violent extremists and had served thirty-five years of a fifty-five-year sentence. It is thought that Oscar López Rivera's release resulted from political pressure and the potential for increased voting power from Puerto Rican democrats. Once released, Oscar López Rivera was honored as a National Freedom Hero at the Puerto Rican Day Parade in NYC on June 9, 2017.

I was and am just as angry as Steven about the release of the FALN members. The thought that two of our presidents released domestic terrorists into society is disgusting. Talk about a threat to US security and the safety of everyone who lives here! How can a president release *terrorists* from prison based on a promise that they will not engage in violence again? Politicians are motivated by votes, not the safety and welfare of American citizens.

In the *New York Daily News* article, Steven said that not a day goes by that the Steinberg family wonders what could have been without the bombing. I could feel his pain.

After reading the article, I felt such a connection to Steven. I was pretty sure that I was the last person who spoke to Charles before the explosion. I felt compelled to contact his brother to express my condolences. I needed closure.

I found Steven's contact information and decided to send him an email.

What do you say to someone you have never met whose brother was killed by the Mobil bombing forty-one years ago?

I wrote from my heart, and on April 19, 2018, I hit send:

Hello. I just came across your name on the internet while I was doing some research for a book I want to write about the FALN bombing of the Mobil Oil Building in 1977...I was working as an intern in the employment office and was probably the last person who spoke to your brother before the explosion...I want to express my sympathy.
Christiane Jane Scarpino

Two days later, I received this response from Steven.

Hi Christiane,
Thanks greatly for your note. It sent chills down my spine. Not a day goes by that I don't think of Charles and what could have been. Our family and my life forever changed on August 3, 1977, as was yours.
Steven Steinberg

In the following days, we transitioned from emails to a phone conversation. This was my first personal connection with someone affected by the Mobil bombing. In forty-plus years, I never felt anyone grasped what had happened and how it changed me. I felt that Steven heard my voice and understood me. Our conversation was both healing and emotional for me. It made me reflect on the value of life and the impact trauma has on family members.

We talked about the day of the Mobil tragedy and how it changed us and continues to affect our lives. I realized what a tremendous shock the loss of Charles was to his family. We honored Charles with our memories of him.

"I always enjoyed Charles's visits to our office. Yes, it was business, but he always had a smile and a funny story to tell," I shared.

I held the phone close to my ear as Steven said, "Charles had a wonderful personality and a great sense of humor. He lit up the room wherever he went."

"Oh yes," I agreed as a tear rolled down my cheek.

"You know, we married sisters. After I married Elizabeth, Charles married her sister, Robin."

"Oh my gosh. Two brothers married two sisters. That's amazing."

My left hand started to squeeze the phone as I spoke.

"That must make it even more difficult for your family...I'm so sorry."

"Charles's death was such a shock to us."

"I'm sure it was. We didn't know where he was after the explosion. We kept asking the police about him but never got an answer," I said, twirling my hair with my right index finger.

Steven continued the conversation.

"Were you hurt? Were you taken to the hospital?"

I pictured myself on the floor of the employment office as I responded.

"I wasn't hurt physically. I found myself across the room, laying at the base of a big potted plant."

Steven added, "We had heard that Charles was propelled across the room, and reportedly, his body protected and saved a woman."

I paused for a moment as I recalled that Charles was standing behind me, next to my desk, between the bomb and my body.

He was watching me walk away. He was the only barrier between me and the bomb.

Charles's body shielded me from the full impact of the explosion.

I shared my surreal realization with Steven.

"The woman Charles protected was me."

CHAPTER 16

WELCOME TO THE FAMILY

I have always wondered why my life was spared. I would not be here today if I hadn't left my desk to get my coffee and bagel. It was a matter of seconds. Learning that Charles took the hit for me filled me with sadness and guilt, even though I had no control over the situation. He was married and had a promising career. He was also a talented musician who played in many Long Island rock groups in the '60s and '70s. I was a young college student who hadn't started to make her mark on the world yet. Maybe he should have lived since he already had a family and a business. I had nothing.

I've figured out that life isn't fair. Tragedy can strike any person at any time, regardless of age, gender, financial status, or life goals. Those things don't matter.

What does matter? Why do some people live and some people die? Is there a predetermined timeline for us?

Is there such a thing as fate? There is a reason for every-thing that happens to us, even if we are unaware of it at the time. Sooner or later, the reason may become apparent if you are open to the knowledge.

I now consider that I have lived my life overcoming trauma so that I can share my story and give others hope in a world that has become more violent. I can be a resil-ient voice for other survivors of violent crimes and their loved ones in the pursuit of supports or services. Every day, I am grateful that I am still alive, although the trauma of the event made my life a nightmare for many years. I have learned to find joy and something positive every day, an attitude that carried me through many difficult years.

Steven and I continued to talk during the next week about how our lives have been affected by the FALN Mobil bombing. Steven told me about someone else whose family was deeply hurt and changed by the FALN. That person was Joe Connor, whose father, Frank Connor, was killed in the FALN bombing of Fraunces Tavern in 1975. Joe was nine years old and wait-ing for his father to come home for his birthday party. Frank Connor never made it home to the party.

Steven shared that Joe had recently coauthored and pub-lished a book in 2018 called *Shattered Lives*, which includes an account of how his family's life had been affected by the Fraunces Tavern bombing. I began to read Joe's book, hop-ing it would help me understand more about the FALN as it applied to my own story. I thought he was an expert on the FALN based on the book's historical content, plus his other publications and numerous public speaking engagements about terrorism. I could only read a little of Joe's book at a time before my eyes blurred with tears. Descriptions of the devastation of the bombing at Fraunces Tavern were so vivid that I could identify with the terror. I would put the book down to give my mind a rest.

I was struck by how this experience was so much like my own. I felt a connection to Joe and decided to contact him. I found his website, We Win America, and sent him a message through the site on April 27, 2018.

Hi Joe,

I recently had a conversation with Steven Steinberg, who told me about you and your book. I feel Steven's and your pain about your losses from the FALN Terrorist attacks, as well as your anger about the release of the FALN Terrorists by Clinton & Obama. I am a survivor of the 1977 FALN bombing of the Mobil Oil Building...

I am thinking about writing a book about reclaiming my life after the terrorist attack. My hope is that it will help others know they can work through the emotional trauma and find some joy in their lives. I am interested in speaking with you to gain insight into the FALN and learn more about your experiences.

Christi Scarpino

The next day, I received this response.

Hello Christi,

Incredible email. Thank you for contacting me. So sorry you had to go through this and carry it for 40 years. You are so brave. How are you physically since the

horror? Would you believe that I worked in that build-
ing for Wells Fargo until January 18? Of all the offices in
NYC...Would be happy to talk or meet as you would like.

Joe

On April 30, Joe and I had our first of many phone conversations.

"Hello, Joe. Thanks for taking the time to speak with me."

"Christi, welcome to the family. You are not alone. I know so many people that have so much in common dealing with these terrorists."

Although I liked his supportive comment, I wasn't sure I liked the idea of "family" in terms of people affected by terrorism.

"I would love to meet others who have experienced the terrorism of the FALN," I responded.

Then, I cleared my throat as I remarked, "I haven't met another person affected by terrorism since the Mobil bombing."

"Unlike the 70s, now there is an amazing network of support."

Where has this amazing network been for the last forty years?

"I've been seeking support and understanding of what I went through on my own," I added.

"You are so brave," Joe said.

"I don't think of myself in that way," I said, slowly shaking my head in disbelief.

"You're so brave for confronting Marie Torres, a terrorist, and grabbing that application from her."

"Well, I didn't know she was a terrorist. I thought she was another weird street person who came into the office to get out of the rain," I said casually.

I dispelled the concept of being brave.

"I was just doing my job, which was to keep people from taking their applications out of the office."

Joe paused and sighed.

"You are underestimating yourself," he exclaimed. "If it weren't for you, the FBI would not have been able to identify Marie Torres because the fingerprints on the application you snatched from her were the *only* evidence."

My forehead wrinkled, signaling my doubt.

"I have always considered myself to be a victim of an unfortunate circumstance," I replied.

"No wonder the FBI was so interested in you. Your actions provided the only evidence *in history* to convict a member of the FALN to a bombing."

I couldn't wrap my head around this. I never realized that I had played such an essential part in the conviction of Marie Torres. I didn't see myself as a hero or brave as Joe did.

Sometimes, we do not see ourselves as others see us.

I had hidden my authentic self from the world for years. People never saw the real me because I kept myself invisible. But Joe, with his understanding of the FALN and how terrorism affects people, saw the real me. I was truly visible to him, and it made me feel vulnerable and safe at the same time.

Joe and I had several more conversations via email and phone.

At the beginning of May, he invited me to the launch of his book, *Shattered Lives*, in Jersey City, New Jersey, later that month. But the launch date was Sunday, May 20, the weekend I was supposed to go to Maine to show dogs. My immediate response was to decline.

This is one of my favorite dog shows. I can't miss it.

The drive to New Jersey will be long and stressful.

I don't think I can be in a room full of people I don't know with terrorism as the main topic of conversation.

I thanked Joe for the invitation and told him I could not make it.

Over the next twenty-four hours, my thinking started to change.

This is an opportunity to meet other people who have been affected by the FALN and other terrorists.

I will get to see two of my favorite views—the NYC skyline and the Statue of Liberty, which I have not seen since I left New York in 1977.

The people there will probably understand what I have been through.

My gut told me that going to Jersey City was something I needed to do. It would be the first time I met anyone else in person who had been affected by terrorism. I would get to meet Joe, who already seemed to be so supportive and understanding. This was a big step forward in my healing journey—being so close to NYC and knowing that the conversations around Joe's book would include terrorism.

There would be triggers, but I thought I could deal with them. I emailed Joe and told him I changed my mind.

✳   ✳   ✳

Over the next few weeks, I canceled my dog show entries and mentally prepared myself for the trip. I found myself becoming more excited by the day—more excitement than anxiety.

I made the six-hour drive to the Hyatt Regency Jersey City on the Hudson in one piece, almost taking the Holland Tunnel by mistake, then cutting across four lanes of traffic to get to my destination.

Once I checked into the hotel, I saw a message from Jeff Ingber, who co-authored *Shattered Lives* with Joe, inviting me to dinner. I unpacked, freshened up, and made my way up the escalator to meet Jeff and Joe for the first time. When I stepped off the escalator, I entered the restaurant, a large room with glass windows revealing the New York City skyline. It was casual but elegant, with square tables covered in tan tablecloths and decorated with a single white candle in the center. All the tables were empty, waiting for guests to arrive, except for one next to the bar. There were three men seated at that table.

That must be Jeff and Joe, but who is the third man?

As I walked towards the table, a tall, balding man who looked to be in his sixties stood up and smiled.

"Christi," he said, extending his hand, "I'm Jeff Ingber."

"Nice to meet you," I responded, shaking his hand.

"This is Joe Connor," he said as he gazed at the middle-aged man on his left.

I made eye contact with Joe to greet him.

"Hello, Joe! Glad to finally meet you!"

Joe stood up and shook my hand.

"It's a pleasure to finally meet you, Christi," said Joe as the corners of his mouth turned up in a smile, exposing his front teeth. "Have a seat."

I sat down, still wondering who the third man was. His aged appearance suggested that he was probably in his mid-seventies, and he obviously had some link to terrorism if he knew Joe.

Jeff looked at me and then glanced at the man, saying, "This is Don Wofford, the FBI Agent who headed the FALN Task Force in the seventies."

For a brief moment, I was in shock.

Why am I sitting with a former FBI agent? This can't be good.

This man's presence blindsided me, as it never occurred to me that an FBI agent would be there. I thought I'd be meeting a supportive group of people, and FBI agents didn't fit that description—at least not to me.

I nodded and put a false smile on my face as I greeted Don.

"Hello, Don. Nice to meet you," I said, although I didn't feel that way.

I sighed deeply and gave a sweeping glance to the men at the table.

"I'm glad to be here. Thank you for inviting me."

We ordered drinks and dinner while conversing about the FALN and the Mobil bombing. They seemed impressed with me, calling me "brave" and a "hero." I felt a little uncomfortable being the center of the conversation.

Just as the waitress brought our dessert and coffee, Joe said, "Marie Torres was the only FALN member that was ever connected to a bombing with evidence, which was her fingerprint on the application that a Mobil employee took from her."

He gazed at me with an astonished expression on his face.

"It's amazing that you are that employee."

"You know you are a hero," Jeff added. "The FBI must have treated you well, knowing that you were the one who could help them convict Marie."

My eyes widened, and I hesitated before choking on my words.

"Ummm. No."

Oh my gosh. They have no idea what happened to me. How could I ever feel like a hero when I was treated like a criminal?

I dropped my fork on the plate with a clang and stared at it.

I then proceeded with a long tirade about how poorly the FBI and the NYPD treated me. Decades of pent-up feelings and pain were pouring out of me, and I could not stop it. There was silence at the table as I heard my loud voice finish with "They were so rude. So disrespectful. They'd interrogate me for hours and never offer me food or water."

My treatment by the authorities equated me with a terrorist.

My monologue left everyone speechless. I felt a pang of guilt for my strong comments to people I had just met, but they were my true feelings. I had a captive audience, and expressing myself to the man who led the FBI task force for the FALN investigation felt good.

Within a few minutes of silence, I felt a hand touching my arm. It was Don Wofford. He broke the silence and the tenseness of the situation with his kind words.

"You did not deserve that treatment."

I looked up at him with tears in my eyes and noticed he also had tears.

"Not all FBI agents were like that. I wish I could prove it to you and make it better."

A few tears escaped down my cheeks. I couldn't find the words to respond, but I think Don knew how much I appreciated his words. He understood how much I was hurting. He understood what I had been through.

At that point, we had all finished our coffee and dessert. Don tapped me on the arm again and said, "Why don't you meet me for breakfast tomorrow?"

"Yes, I will," I responded as I got up from the table and returned to my room.

✷   ✷   ✷

I awoke Sunday morning to a beautiful sunny day. I threw on my running clothes and went for a jog on the hard pavement alongside New York Harbor. I could see the NYC skyline to my left as I ran, intending to see Lady Liberty on my run. It was my time to daydream and clear my head, as running always allowed me to do. I admired the skyscrapers and the grayness of the water, with the breeze making ripples in the harbor. Seeing the outline of New York City felt good to me. I did not feel anxious or upset. It was almost comforting as it reminded me of my roots.

I finished my run, showered, and met Don for breakfast. There's nothing like enjoying New York bagels and coffee while discussing the FALN. This time, the conversation was not about me. Don shared stories about his life and work with the FBI. His was an entirely different perspective, and I listened intently as I learned how difficult it was to apprehend these terrorists.

He seemed compassionate, unlike the other FBI agents I had interacted with.

Just as we finished breakfast, he touched my arm and said, "I feel so bad about how FBI agents treated you...On behalf of the entire FBI, I apologize."

Don made me feel like I was valued, unlike the FBI agents I had interacted with in the '70s. This breakfast took me full circle. The last time I had New York bagels and coffee was the day of the Mobil bombing, which marked the first day of my poor relationship with the FBI. There I was, forty-one years later, having a New York bagel and coffee with the FBI agent who led the task force against the FALN.

A few hours later, we walked to a restaurant for a luncheon to celebrate the launch of Joe's book. We were led to a private room, big enough for about thirty people. We were seated around a long, rectangular table. All the people sitting around the table were connected to terrorist attacks somehow, as lawyers, former FBI agents, NYPD officers, survivors of the Fraunces Tavern explosion, first responders and survivors of the 9/11 terrorist attack in NYC, and people who had lost loved ones and family members from a terrorist attack. After we were seated at the table, Joe stood beside me.

"Everyone," he said, putting his hand on my shoulder, "We have a new guest here."

"This is Christi Scarpino. She survived the FALN bombing of the Mobil Employment Office in 1977."

I glanced around at the men and women sitting at the table, responding with, "It's an honor to be here."

I thought the introduction was over, but Joe continued.

"Christi is the woman who took the employment application from Marie Torres. Her actions produced the only piece of evidence that linked any FALN member to a bombing and caused Marie Torres to be convicted."

I could feel my cheeks becoming hot with embarrassment. I did not like being the center of attention.

"I needed to keep that application in the office for statistics," I said. "I had no idea she was a terrorist."

"You were very brave to confront her."

I really did do something important...

Yet, I still do not see myself as brave. I see myself as having my identity stripped because I was treated like a prisoner by the authorities and had very little control over my life.

The people seated around the table wore welcoming smiles and nodded in agreement about my bravery. Their eyes told me that although they saw me as brave, they also saw me as someone who had suffered. I felt seen and heard, although I said very little.

As lunch was served, I spoke to many strong people who had experienced a loss due to terrorism. Conversation revolved around how terrorism had impacted our lives, remembering and sometimes reliving the trauma every day. I realized that I was not alone anymore. I was with a group of people who inherently understood me and what my life had been like.

I was a teardrop away from uncontrollable sobbing when I heard the stories of other people. There was so much compassion and empathy in that small space. Eye contact was all that was needed to share and acknowledge emotions.

Just as dessert and coffee were being served, Joe and Jeff stood up at the end of the table.

Jeff spoke first.

"I'd like to thank everyone for coming today to celebrate with us. You all contributed somehow to the book, which we appreciate."

Joe added, "We are all in this together. You are part of the story and the reason we wrote the book. We need justice served for the FALN terrorists for the deaths of our family members and friends."

The connections I made at the book launch had a profound impact on me, and I no longer felt like I was alone.

My feelings were validated, and the experience seemed to fill some emotional gaps inside me. I had more ideas for my book as a result of the weekend.

The six-hour drive home late Sunday afternoon seemed to go quickly, as I was preoccupied with thoughts about the weekend. I felt such solidarity, strength, kindness, and support from people I had just met. I felt a strange sense of peace and unspoken deep connections. I will never forget it. That weekend was a major victory for my reconnection to the world and, more importantly, a reconnection to myself and understanding who I am.

I am braver than I ever knew.

CHAPTER 17

STRONGER

Bill and I continued to date when he was home, and when he was at sea, we would talk via Zoom every night. There were no more bomb threats or threats of violence at work. Nobody was sick. Nobody died. I was sleeping well, and nothing was triggering PTSD reactions.

Life was good.

In March 2019, Bill was invited to a friend's birthday celebration in Hawaii in July. Most people there would be people he worked with on the cruise ship, the U.S.S. Constitution, the ship we met on in 1988. He invited me to accompany him.

I was delighted to go and accepted his invitation without any anxiety about airports. We made our travel reservations, which included three days in Honolulu and four days in Kauai.

After attending the birthday celebration in Honolulu, we flew to Kauai, where we stayed in a new hotel that was not completed, which was not evident on their website. The restaurant was not open, the spa was not finished, and the pool had no water. That being a disappointment, we spent most of our time away from the hotel.

We did lots of sightseeing and challenged ourselves with ziplining. Bill had made reservations for dinner at a friend's restaurant one night. We had a delicious Italian meal overlooking the beach. After dinner, we went for a walk along the coast as Bill wanted to show me where the ship had docked when we met. We walked hand-in-hand, enjoying the soft, warm breeze. It reminded me of our evening walk in Ashburnham when we realized we still had feelings for one another.

"It's a full moon tonight," he said as we strolled on the beachside path. "Too bad there is so much cloud cover we can't see the moon."

"It's beautiful, just the same," I replied. "It would be nice if there was lighting along the walkway, however."

"I know where we are going," Bill said as we walked up a little hill.

When we reached the top of the hill, I could see a lighthouse lit up below us.

Bill stopped and faced me. Now holding both my hands, he looked down into my eyes and said, "This is exactly where we met."

My heart was beating a little faster, and I wanted to remember this moment of silence in the pitch-black evening, with the only light being the beam from the light-house. The gentle breeze tickled my cheeks and blew a little hair into my eyes.

"Christiane Jane Scarpino...."

I gently swept the hair away so I could see him clearly.

"Will you marry me?"

Looking up at Bill, I could feel his love and knew he was the one for me. Our connection was still strong thirty-one years after we met in this very spot.

"Yes," I said softly, lovingly.

He pulled a small, navy-blue box from his pocket, opened it, and showed me a round, brilliant-cut diamond ring that sparkled in the darkness. The halo setting and dia-monds on the band added to its brilliance. Bill took my left hand and slipped it onto my ring finger.

We put our arms around one another and kissed with the full moon's light, now peeking through the clouds.

We turned around and slowly found our way back to the restaurant. We walked in silence, arm-in-arm, just relishing the beauty of the evening as a newly engaged couple.

It was a perfect evening and the end of a perfect trip. It was a love story that went full circle in Kauai, resulting in our decision to spend our lives together. This was a new beginning for me. It was time to go home to spread the news of our engagement and plan our future.

Once we arrived home, we announced our engagement to family and friends. Some were surprised, but most were not. Everyone was happy for us. We started discussing wed-ding plans, as Bill would return to sea in a couple of weeks.

I knew that wedding planning takes time, and starting earlier rather than later was best. Bill suggested that our wedding date be the same as my birthday (so he had a better chance of remembering the dates). I would have rather we eloped, but since it was his first marriage, a wedding with friends and family present was important to him. We agreed to set our wedding date two years away on August 13, 2021.

August of 2019 came and went, and I realized I did not have an anniversary reaction that year! Perhaps the excitement of our engagement had something to do with it. That was the second year since the bombing that I hadn't noticed any reaction around the anniversary date.

Over the years, my reaction had changed to lethargy and mild anxiety, but it did not interfere with my ability to function. I didn't even notice these subtle reminders in 2019. I was feeling so much better, and I was sure I was almost cured of my PTSD symptoms. I hadn't had any responses to triggers in over a year!

Bill was away from August through December 2019, during which time I was busy with work and planning our wedding. I secured a venue in New Jersey, entertainment, a photographer, and a florist and found a dress. The major things were taken care of, which was great because, in March 2020, the deadly COVID-19 virus shut the world down. Restaurants, service businesses, hotels, and many stores were closed. There could be no gatherings with large numbers of people, such as church services and weddings, because these functions would likely spread the virus. We could only hope that this would not impact our wedding, which was sixteen months away.

One good thing about 2020? I did not notice an anniversary reaction for the third year in a row...

* * *

In early 2021, stores, hotels, and services started slowly opening up with restrictions. Bill was at sea until July, so I had to manage all the wedding details from Massachusetts. Our wedding venue was the Gate House at the Old Mill Inn in Basking Ridge, New Jersey.

Three months before the wedding, I sold my house in Massachusetts, stored all my worldly goods, and got ready (with the dogs) to move to New Jersey. It made sense for me to move since Bill was building a house there, and I had been thinking about leaving Ashburnham even before Bill and I got engaged. Between selling my primary residence and relocating to New Jersey, I stayed in my summer cottage in Ashburnham.

Bill came home in July, just in time to get our marriage license and help with final arrangements and payments. Then, the first few days of August slipped by without any evidence of my PTSD. It was a busy, happy time, which overshadowed my difficult past. This was the fourth year in a row without an anniversary reaction. This must mean I'm cured.

I stayed at the Old Mill Inn a few days before the wedding. Friday morning, August 13, I woke up early and met my niece, Miri, and friend, Bonnie, who were my bridesmaids. I splurged and had our makeup and hair done by local stylists while our photographer was in our midst recording the results.

It was a beautiful, sunny day, which turned out to be the hottest day of the summer at over ninety degrees. Our ceremony was outside, in front of a white gazebo adorned with summer wildflowers—reds, purples, whites, and greens over the top and down the sides of the gazebo. A basket of flowers was placed at the end of each row of the white seats for our guests. At 4:00 p.m., our guests were greeted by hotel staff with a choice of lemonade or iced tea and escorted to their seats in front of the gazebo. The beautiful sounds of the harpist's melodies serenaded our guests for the ceremony. Bill and his two groomsmen, dressed in gray suits with purple bow ties and boutonnieres, walked down the cobblestone path to the gazebo one by one. Next came my niece, Miri, and friend, Bonnie, each wearing a different style of floor-length purple dress. As they all were standing in front of the gazebo, it was now the bride's turn, my turn, to walk down the cobblestone path.

People told me I looked stunning in my Maggie Sottero ivory lace fit-and-flare dress. It had a sweetheart neckline and illusion back with a layer of blush satin beneath the lace. Walking down the cobblestone path, I was careful not to catch my heels in the crevices. I smiled as I slowly walked toward Bill with my four-foot train behind me, spreading its dainty lace over the cobblestones. My hair was neatly styled in a bun, with a floral band adorning my head.

I don't think I've ever felt this beautiful before.

I reached the gazebo, and Bill and I faced each other as the officiant started the ceremony. We said our vows, which we had each written down in a small keepsake booklet. I went first.

"Thank you for showing up. I never doubted you, but you did mention that you might send a clown or a clone."

I could hear laughter from our guests.

"I knew you'd be here for me, and I promise to always be there for you."

I looked up at Bill, and as our eyes met, I said tenderly, "Here's a few reasons why I love you...You are kind, caring, loving, sincere, a little smart, and very sarcastic..." A soft smile spread across his face as I quickly added, "You are also quirky, and my dogs adore you."

Bill chuckled, fully aware of the importance of having my dogs' acceptance.

I took a step forward and put my hands around his.

"I promise to cultivate flexibility, communication, understanding, and sarcasm, and whatever else it takes for us to flourish as a couple and maintain our individuality."

I gently squeezed Bill's hands.

"You're the person I want to spend the rest of my life with."

I released Bill's hands and stepped back, signaling it was his turn to say his vows to me. He shifted his weight while his facial expression turned more serious. He looked into my eyes and spoke softly.

"I look forward to a life together as we head towards retirement..."

His face was moist from the heat and humidity, and he wiped his brow with his handkerchief.

"...Our love for each other has grown over the years. The distances between us and the pandemic have added challenges, but we have managed to move ahead...No doubt we will make a great team."

I felt droplets in the corners of my eyes, not from the heat but from the sound of love in his voice.

Bill touched my hands with certainty as he finished his vows.

"I do promise to have and to hold, for better and for worse, for richer and for poorer, in sickness and in health until death do us part."

A large smile illuminated Bill's face, and he declared, "And finally, I promise to be more prompt than the nearly twenty years that passed between the first time I told you I would call you and when I actually did."

We both said, "I do," and embarked on a new chapter in our lives. We turned around and walked down the cobblestone path, caressed by the late afternoon breeze, arm-in-arm to start our life together. Our forty guests followed us into the reception hall, where we celebrated with a gourmet dinner and dancing. It was the most memorable day of my life because I finally had a partner who understood and accepted me for who I was, and I had someone special to share my newly discovered self with. Together, we would walk the path of self-discovery as a couple, allowing me to continue flourishing in my evolving identity.

✳   ✳   ✳

Bill went back to sea a couple of months after our wedding. He had not retired yet and was still returning to sea every four to six months and coming home for the same amount of time. I was unsure if I wanted to return to work after dealing with COVID-19 for the past two years. I spent the next four months unpacking and settling the dogs in their new home. I focused on writing my memoir since I had the time.

In January 2022, Bill was home again, but only for a month. It was hard for me and the dogs to adjust to this lifestyle of having him home inconsistently and living in a new place where I had no friends or family. Around this time, my niece, who lived in Europe, was visiting NYC on business and asked if we could meet her in the city. I had no idea how to get into the city from our Ringwood, New Jersey home, and asked Bill, who volunteered to come with me.

I was excited about going to NYC but a little nervous about taking public transportation. There had been a shooting in the subway a month before, which reminded me that violence can be anywhere. I had experienced very few PTSD

symptoms over the past two to three years, but I was concerned that I might become overly anxious and experience
some symptoms once back in the city. I wanted to be cau-
tious, and Bill respected that. I was happy to have Bill come
with me to help in case I became anxious and panicked.

With Bill as my travel escort, I felt safe. Knowing he was
with me and I was not alone made me feel confident about
the trip. He drove to a ferry terminal, where we boarded the
ferry and went to NYC. We walked several blocks to meet
my niece for lunch on the chilly but otherwise perfect day.
I had no anxiety once in New York, to my surprise. I didn't
worry about terrorists or violence.

✳   ✳   ✳

Bill returned to sea in February, and Turner passed away
in March. With my husband at sea and Turner gone, I felt
alone. I still had two Tollers, Nadia, age twelve, and Alden,
age seven. They were both getting older and retired from
competition. Alden had turned into Bill's dog, and Nadia was
non-committal. I was lonely and wanted another dog to train.
Shortly after Bill returned home in August, Encore came into
our lives. He is so much like Turner that I think that Turner
picked him for me. My life became busy with puppy training,
and I spent the remainder of 2022 enjoying my new puppy
while Bill was at sea again. The year 2022 turned out to be
another year free of PTSD symptoms with no anniversary
reactions. Again, I thought my PTSD was cured.

I hunkered down in 2023 to finish writing the first draft of my memoir. I worked on it sporadically but got a lot done when I stayed at my summer cottage in Ashburnham. Sometimes, it was tough for me to write about my life after the bombing, but I was also surprised that it didn't trigger me. August 3, 2023, came and went, and I didn't notice any changes in my demeanor.

Bill came home from sea over the summer, and we planned to see Bruce Springsteen in concert on August 30. I saw Bruce perform at the Rutgers University Student Activities Center in the '70s for fifty cents admission. I was excited about seeing him in a real concert now that he was famous.

I knew there would be crowds and noise, but I thought I could handle it. I had tested the waters of PTSD reactions with other concerts in the past couple of years and had no issues: We had seen The Rolling Stones, Paul McCartney, and Ed Sheeran.

The concert was at the MetLife Stadium in East Rutherford, New Jersey. We left late in the afternoon for the performance that started at 7:00 p.m. Bill was driving since I had no clue how to get there. To our surprise, as we got off the highway exit, traffic was backed up for miles.

We crept along at five miles per hour until we reached the stadium forty-five minutes later. Then, seven traffic lanes merged into three to enter the parking lot.

My stomach started to feel queasy, and I knew Bill was aggravated.

"This is crazy!" I said. "Look at all the people going to this concert!"

"Once we find a place to park, it'll get better," he said, gripping the steering wheel.

Several stadium employees directed us to one of the parking lots. People were everywhere, engaging in pre-concert parties with no regard for anyone else, especially for people wanting to park their cars. We drove up and down several lanes until, finally, a stadium employee made people move their chairs and grill so we could park.

"These people are drunk way before the concert! How will they possibly enjoy it?"

"Maybe they think they will enjoy it more," Bill said.

Maybe we're just getting old, I thought.

We got out of our car, took a photo of the landmarks around it (so we could find it later), and headed towards the stadium entrance. There were at least ten long lines at the entrance with people showing their digital tickets, putting their personal items through the scanner, and, in some cases, being scanned with wands.

"Lots of security for this one," I commented. "Do you think they are worried about violence?"

"They probably are more concerned about people bringing in water bottles and forbidden food items," Bill said.

"In one sense, the heightened security makes me feel safer, but on the other hand, I have to wonder if there is something particular they are looking for or thinking they might find."

We took a few more baby steps closer to the ticket offices.

"If you're thinking about a bomb, I doubt there's any concern," Bill assured me.

I wasn't sure how he could be so certain about this. His comment reminded me that the probability of a bomb was low. However, I knew that the possibility was always there. My anxiety was raised a couple of notches, but I could deal with it. Or so I thought.

We were now standing in front of the ticket officials and synced our digital tickets from our phones to their tablets. We were then admitted and directed to our seats in area 132. I had selected that area because it was close to the stairwell and only one flight up. We'd be among the first to get out if the stadium was evacuated. I didn't mind paying more money to be closer to the exit. I don't think Bill agreed with me, but he tolerated my behavior because he knew it made me feel safer. Even if he didn't totally understand some of my over-cautious behaviors, he was tolerant and accepting of them.

We made our way to our seats, and it was an hour before the concert was set to begin. There were people crowded in the aisles, moving about, then climbing over me with their drinks. It was uncomfortable, and there was no personal space. A big man who was overflowing in his seat sat to my right. Bill was sitting to my left. He could see I was getting stressed.

"Do you want something to eat? To drink?" he asked.

"Good idea. I'll have some fried clams with tartar sauce and one of those strawberry margaritas."

"OK. Let's go. The concession stand is close to the stairwell."

"You go. I am not getting out of my seat and climbing over all these people. You know I hate crowds. People never see me, and I get pushed around. I'm staying put."

While Bill was getting our food and my drink, I was overwhelmed by how full the stadium was of people. In past concerts at other venues, there were always vacant seats around us. That night, every seat seemed to be filled well before the concert. As the aroma of pot circled beneath my nose, I realized that people were both drunk and stoned. I started watching the pre-concert announcements on the gigantic screen by the stage. The screen turned bright red as the loudspeaker emitted these words:

ATTENTION EVERYONE.

IN CASE OF EVACUATION, HERE IS THE PLAN.

Then, the screen listed the order of evacuation, floor by floor, section by section, and row by row.

Oh my God. They think there's going to be a problem

Waves of anxiety came over my body. I took deep breaths.

Bill came back with our snacks. There was nothing like soggy fried clams and the worst margarita I had ever tasted.

The lights dimmed, and the curtain went up at 8:00 p.m., revealing the E Street Band and The Boss himself, Bruce Springsteen. The band started playing, and people stood up, waved their arms, and started screaming. The man sitting next to me hit me in the cheek with his elbow as he stood up. He didn't apologize. I don't think he even noticed. My cheek was throbbing, and I was overwhelmed with sensory overload within the first fifteen minutes of the concert.

The piercing sound of the band's guitars was deafening. The sounds were reverberating in my head. I couldn't even make out what Springsteen was playing.

The lights. Glaring, blinking, changing color, and blinding me.

The music beat and the flashing lights' rhythm competed against one another.

People were shouting the lyrics of the songs.

I put my hands over my ears.
My ears are going to explode.

I tucked my chin and looked down to avoid seeing the flashing lights.
Those lights are so harsh. What are they trying to do to people?

I buried my eyes in my left forearm and covered my head with my sweater.
I feel a little better.

Bill looked at me and didn't say anything.
I stayed in this position for a good thirty minutes and then decided to sit up.
Bad idea.
My senses were immediately deluged with the intensity of sound and light and the smells of pot and cigarette smoke.

"Bill."

No response. He didn't hear me.

"Bill," I said a little louder as I tapped him on the shoulder.

He turned and looked at me.

"I need to get up. This is too much for me."

"What?" he shouted back.

I pointed to the exit and made walking signs with my fingers. He nodded, and I got up and went into the corridor.

I walked over to one of the concession stands and leaned against the wall. I took deep breaths and told myself I was going to be OK. All I wanted to do was get out of there.

After about thirty minutes, I saw Bill walking towards me.

"Are you OK?" he asked.

"No, it's too much for me in there. I can't go back in."

"Do you think you'll feel better?"

"We can wait a bit and find out," I said out of politeness. I didn't want to wait. I wanted to leave. But I didn't want Bill to miss the concert either.

We both leaned up against the wall in silence.

Bill looked at me. "Don't you feel well? What's wrong?"

I thought he had figured it out, but apparently, he had not. "I'm on overload, and I feel like my head is going to explode. Standing in line, the crowds, the evacuation plan, the flashing lights, and the noise. It feels so out of control."

"Well, I don't think I understand."

"I don't want to feel this way. I can't help it."

"Do you want to go back in and try again?"

"Are you kidding me? There's no way I can go back in there."

My eyes filled up with tears.

Another half an hour of standing stiffly against the wall in silence.

It was now close to ten p.m., and I wondered how much longer I would have to stand there.

I turned to face Bill.

"I want to leave."

He sighed, "Okay."

We turned together and walked down the stairs to exit the building.

"I'm really sorry. I just can't stay."

We walked along, staring straight ahead, although I did notice a few people standing outside.

Perhaps it was too noisy in there for them, too.

A sense of relief flooded my body as we got to our car: no lines, no people, no music, and no flashing lights. I was starting to feel better.

Bill drove us home, and we didn't say much about the evening. I apologized a couple of times, as I felt so guilty about ruining Bill's concert experience.

The next day, after reading reviews of the concert online, I tried initiating a conversation with Bill about it while we sat next to each other at the dinner table.

"The concert is getting mixed reviews," I shared as I dipped my spoon in a bowl of tomato soup. "What did you think?"

Bill looked up from his bowl and said, "I thought it was great, but you obviously didn't."

I put my spoon down and wiped some tomato soup off my lips. "I thought it was loud. I couldn't tolerate those flashing lights."

"I could see that."

"I really tried to sit through it. I'm sorry I ruined the concert for you."

Bill slurped some soup from his spoon. "I'll get over it."

Our conversation ended there, and it felt unresolved to me. I still felt guilty. I realized that although Bill had commented that he understood my PTSD, he didn't. He had heard me talk about it but had never experienced it. Knowing someone with PTSD and living with someone with PTSD are very different.

* * *

A few months later, the topic of the concert came up when I was talking about finishing my memoir. We were on the phone as Bill was at sea.

"How's the book going? Are you almost done with the first draft?" he asked.

"I'm writing about us now—our engagement, our wedding, and how good I was doing until the Springsteen concert."

"I wish you would get better."

My mouth dropped open as this comment took me aback.

"I AM better," I said emphatically.

I suddenly realized that Bill did not know me well when I was at my worst, struggling to get through the day. He had no idea how incapacitated I used to be and had no basis for comparison.

"I mean TOTALLY better," he explained. "No more PTSD reactions."

I let out a big sigh and said, "I know we both thought that I was cured because I have not had any PTSD reactions for a few years. But the concert experience proved that wrong. I think we're both going to have to accept that PTSD reactions will always be a part of me. My reactions used to be so frequent and severe that I could barely get through the day. Now I am pretty functional except when my system gets overloaded with triggers like what happened at the concert."

After a short pause, he said, "I guess you're right. We can deal with it."

"Yes," I replied. "We're a strong team."

CHAPTER 18

TAKING MY LIFE BACK

In October of 2023, while Bill was at work out at sea, I was working hard to finish my memoir's first draft. I still wasn't employed but retained my license to practice speech-language pathology "just in case" I decided to return to work. I volunteered two days per week, training dogs at a local shelter. I spent the rest of my time training Encore, my young dog following in Turner's footsteps. I noticed that my focus had changed with my dogs.

I was now training my dogs for enjoyment rather than distracting myself from anxiety and intrusive thoughts. I had gotten well enough to let that coping strategy go and just enjoy having dogs. Instead, training them had become an activity I enjoyed and did to please myself. Although it is satisfying to achieve titles with your dog, it is not a goal of mine anymore.

Encore is a lot like Turner. He is just as smart and thinks he knows it all. When you have a dog like that, you need to keep them busy and always stay one or two steps ahead of them. Turner trained himself to be my service dog for my PTSD reactions. I started training Encore to be my service dog for other reasons. My osteoarthritis and osteoporosis had begun to limit my mobility sometimes, and I trained Encore to pick things up off the floor and get specific objects for me, such as my phone. I hope he will be my companion and service dog for the next decade or longer.

* * *

In December 2023, I finished my manuscript and was looking for feedback. I wasn't confident it was good enough to publish, so I asked Joe Connor to read it. Joe agreed, and I sent him a copy to read. He extended an invitation to join him and a group of people for lunch at Fraunces Tavern in NYC on January 24, 2024, the anniversary date of the FALN bombing. People who have been affected by terrorism gather there every year for lunch as an opportunity to check in with and support one another. I accepted Joe's invitation.

On the morning of January 24, I drove to Joe's house thirty minutes away, and we took the train and the Path together into NYC with another friend of Joe's. We chatted on the train ride, and I was secretly amazed at how calm I felt.

We transferred to the subway and walked to Fraunces Tavern on this chilly January day. We were escorted to a reserved table in the Bissell Room close to the commemorative plaque for Frank Connor and the 1975 bombing of the tavern. There was an amazing mural depicting the New York Harbor in 1717. A long crack runs through the middle of the mural due to the bombing, bringing the reality of the explosion to the present day. But more amazing was the conversation and the company. There were people there who had lost family members from terrorism, survivors of 9/11, police officers, and firefighters.

About ten of us were seated around the rectangular table in the corner of the room. We ordered our meals and chatted about our experiences with terrorism. As I dug into the gigantic salad I had ordered, I shared my story about the Mobil bombing. The room became quiet, and all eyes were on me when I mustered up the courage to say, "I just finished the first draft of my book about the Mobil bombing and my lifelong struggle with PTSD."

"That's amazing!" exclaimed one of the police officers.

"I'm not sure anyone will want to read it," I replied.

Joe chimed in, "Are you kidding? I've read parts of the draft. It's so raw and interesting. You need to publish it."

Others at the table nodded their heads in agreement.

"Your story needs to be told," said one of the 9/11 first responders.

I feel empowered to publish my book.

Feeling more confident, I added, "Well, now I will have to figure out how to get it published. I will do this!"

After lunch, we walked to the 9/11 Memorial since it was on the way to the subway station. I had never been there before and felt compelled to see it. It started pouring rain, and Joe and I shared a small black umbrella to keep dry. The memorial itself was overwhelming to me. To stand in the place where the Twin Towers stood, realizing how many people were in there and lost their lives, was just devastating. I could almost visualize the buildings crumbling and falling to the ground, seeing the thick air and the devastation. I was hurting for other people's losses.

Later, I realized I had not responded to two of my "old" triggers—the rain and a collapsible black umbrella like the one the bomb was in. I was more affected by the sadness of the 9/11 tragedy, and I realized I was feeling so much empathy for anyone connected with it. My responses were proof of the progress I had made in handling triggers and feeling emotion.

* * *

In July 2024, I was working on my manuscript at my summer cottage. I had spent the morning writing and had been writing about the loss of my diamond and ruby teardrop necklace—the necklace that was my reminder that I was alive and safe. I decided to take a break and go into Fitchburg to Duvarney's Jewelers, where I had been buying jewelry for over thirty years. Bill told me I could pick something out as an early anniversary and birthday present, and he agreed that I could buy myself a necklace and a pair of earrings from Duvarney's.

I drove to Main Street and parked in the municipal lot across the street from the jewelry shop. I crossed the street and opened the glass door to enter.

As I walked in, I was greeted by Steve Duvarney, dressed impeccably in a dark suit. Steve's grandfather owned the business for many years, and then Steve took it over.

"Hi Christi. Good to see you. What can I do for you today?"

"I'm here to look for my birthday and anniversary presents from Bill," I responded.

"Smart man," he said, smiling. "Is there anything in particular you are looking for?"

"Well, I'd like a necklace with a sapphire or a pink tourmaline. I'd like something in rose gold and earrings, too."

As Steve shuffled around behind the glass cases in search of items that matched my desires, he asked, "How's everything going? Are you still working, or did you retire?"

"Well," I responded, "I decided it was time to retire from speech-language pathology, although I still have my license to practice."

I bent down to look into the cases as we chatted.

"However, I have a full-time job doing something else. I'm writing my memoir."

"Really? I'm fascinated," he said. "Tell me about it."

And then, to my surprise, the words just flowed out of my mouth.

"I don't know if I ever told you," I said, knowing I hadn't. "But I am a survivor of a terrorist bombing in NYC in 1977."

"Did you have PTSD?" he asked.

"Yes," I asserted. "I still do! One of my hopes is that my memoir will help people understand how PTSD affects people and create awareness of the need for more services for all people who are survivors of severe trauma."

"You're doing so well now with talking about it," he said. "I want to read your book. When do you think it will be published?"

"Hopefully by late 2025," I stated, proud that I just plugged my book. "Now, let's look at some jewelry!"

At first, Steve pointed out a lovely sapphire necklace, but it didn't sing to me.

I moved over to the next case of jewels. A particular necklace caught my eye towards the back of the case.

"Can I see that one?" I asked as I pointed to the necklace that I was attracted to.

I stopped breathing for a few seconds as Steve unlocked the glass display case and put the necklace gently on a pad of black velvet on the counter for me to see.

There it was—an 18K rose gold chain with two stones hanging from it. At the top was a round, 2.5 mm round cut diamond and a 10 mm pink tourmaline teardrop hanging below it. It was the same design as the necklace I had lost, only bigger, stronger, and more beautiful. It was also a little different. The ruby, a symbol of strength, energy, and vitality, was replaced by a pink tourmaline, a symbol of love, compassion, and emotional healing. The diamond was five times the size of the original, giving more power to its representation of strength, resilience, invincibility, and eternal love.

I whipped out my credit card, not even considering the price.

"I'll take it. Do you have earrings that would match?"

Steve took a minute to look at the earrings in the adjacent display case. He unlocked it and placed a small, dark blue rectangular box with gold trim on the display case.

I opened the box and gasped in delight. My eyes twinkled with the vision of 18k white gold drop earrings, each with a round, red tourmaline surrounded by five round diamonds.

Steve always knows what I like.

"Would you like to try them on?" Steve asked.

I gave a little grin. "That won't be necessary. These are perfect."

And again, with no regard to the price tag, "Wrap them up, too, please."

What are the chances that I would find the same necklace design *after* I had written about the loss of the original one that morning? What are the chances that Steve would show this necklace to me shortly after we spoke about my memoir?

This is more than a coincidence. This is a sign from the Universe that I have found the missing pieces.

I got the greatest gift from the Universe.

I am strong.

I am resilient.

I am the diamond and the tourmaline.

I am alive.

I am fine just the way I am—whole and imperfect.

EPILOGUE: I AM WHOLE

My journey is not finished. It is only the beginning because as I completed the final chapters of this memoir, I realized how much more I have to share. This was confirmed when I went to an author's workshop to improve my skills towards the end of drafting. We did an exercise to tap into our higher intuition (or self) using the Sacred Rebels Oracle Deck.

I wasn't familiar with these cards then, but the approach was one to celebrate and nurture your individuality and creativity and identify your power. Everyone in the workshop randomly chose a card and then had to relate the message on the card with their experience as a writer or see what message the oracle might offer about their authorial journey or the book they were writing. The card I drew was "Visions of Life Before Death."

Wow! What an amazing connection to my thoughts about life and death while writing this book. I was close to being killed in the explosion. I would not have been telling this story if I had not walked away from my desk to get a cup of coffee and bagel. I still wonder why my life was spared. I wonder why some people live long lives, and others leave the earth at a young age. I wonder what my purpose is. Picking that card held too much truth to be coincidental! As I learned more about the meaning of this card, I understood the truths that this card held for me.

It indicated that I had outgrown my old version of self to embrace a new, better self. My old self was gone, and I had gained a new, stronger self. I had found my identity. My perspective had shifted, and I was gaining true insight into myself. I knew who I was. The rest of the card's description concluded that accepting and loving who I am today enables me to live joyfully.

So powerful.

So true.

The card indicated that my increased insight allows me to share my experience in meaningful ways to help others. Writing *Missing Pieces* is the first step in my mission to improve others' understanding of PTSD and the long-term effects of trauma. My original manuscript contained much more detail about how I managed my memory loss, anxiety, and panic attacks over the years. As I started editing, I realized that that information really didn't belong in my memoir. However, it has value for people navigating PTSD and is better suited for a self-help book. At the time of this writing, the outline for that book has begun.

With my combined background and experience as a speech-language pathologist and massage therapist, blended with my forty-five years' experience living with PTSD, the next book promises to be a resource full of strategies that a person can use to enhance their daily living and become more functional. To this day, I utilize many of the strategies to make my days more peaceful and productive.

I also have plans to increase public awareness of PTSD through podcasts, public speaking, and online forums. My biggest dream would be to help people with their memory, organization, and planning problems as a result of their PTSD based on my training as a speech-language pathologist and from my personal experience.

PTSD is not just feeling sad, depressed, or overwhelmed. It certainly can encompass those components, but it is so much more. It's one of those silent mental illnesses that everybody talks about, but few people acknowledge. You can lose your sense of identity, your memory, and your purpose for living. It's not easy to live with, not easy to talk about, and not easily understood by others. As a result, PTSD becomes a silent battle for an individual. I have learned that you can't erase your trauma, but you can change how you respond to it. Similarly, for those who do not have PTSD but have not tried to empathize or opted instead to make judgments, you, too, can (and should) change how you respond to someone with PTSD.

Instead of asking, "What's wrong with them?" try asking, "How can I support them?"

For many years, I struggled with who I was and felt like I lost control of my life. There is hope, and you can get better. The Mobil bombing changed me in many ways, but it no longer haunts me or controls me. I am now in control. You too, can gain control of your life.

I changed. I'm still changing. I'm not avoiding myself anymore. I'm in love with my changing self. I know who I am. I feel emotions again. I fell in love. My day-to-day memory is back. I'm a calmer person but still energetic. I only do things that bring me joy. I have found community with other people who have been affected by terrorism. How ironic that I have established friendships with people connected to an experience I wish had never happened.

I've worked hard to find myself. The time and effort it took to get me to this place was worth it.

Life is good.

I am no longer broken.

I have found the missing pieces.

ACKNOWLEDGMENTS

Many people have played a significant role in my recovery from PTSD, and those who have encouraged me to tell my story. I can't name everyone but know that if you have been a part of my life, I am thankful for you.

First and foremost, I thank my mother, who continues to be with me in spirit. She taught me to be a strong, resilient woman and to use my talents wisely, and she inspired my creativity. Most importantly, she gave me her positive attitude and encouraged me to believe in myself. I also thank my older siblings, Jon, Guy, and Karin, for being a support system for their baby sister over the years. To my father, I wish you could have understood me better and accepted my opinions, but I learned the art of disagreeing and self-advocating from you.

To the NYPD Bomb Squad, I thank you for rescuing me from the rubble after the bomb explosion on August 3, 1977.

To the FBI agents responsible for apprehending the FALN terrorists and putting them behind bars, I thank you for seeking justice for their violent acts.

Thank you to Dr. Claudia Siebel, the psychologist I saw for thirty years. You helped me through some dark times and always made me feel safe (although sometimes you asked me questions that made me uncomfortable).

Thank you to Dr. Neil Castronovo, the psychologist who helped me find the final missing pieces and put my flashbacks to rest with EMDR. You also deserve thanks for encouraging me to write a book to share my story.

To my friend, Bonnie Keveaney, who always took the time to listen to me, understood my emotional pain without judgment, and suggested EMDR, thank you from the bottom of my heart.

I will always be grateful to all my Boston Terriers and my Toller, Turner (whose AKC registered, titled name was CH HR Edlyn Seastar Turn of Events, UD, SH, WCX, CGC, VC) for the special bond we had. You will always be my heart dog.

Special thanks to Steven Steinberg for sharing what a wonderful person his brother Charles was and the impact that his murder by terrorists had on his family. Charles will never be forgotten.

My deep appreciation goes to Joe Connor for his validation of my story, encouraging me to tell it, and helping me realize my contribution to history in the fight against terrorism. Thank you for introducing me to other people affected by terrorism, as the strength of this community has helped me to heal.

Thank you to Don Wofford, former FBI agent. Although he is no longer with us, I will always appreciate his global apology for the way the FBI treated me during my interrogations.

To Steve Duvarney of Duvarney Jewelers, thank you for supplying me with wonderful jewelry for many years, especially the pink tourmaline teardrop necklace.

Thank you to my beta readers, Lyudmyla Hoffman, Tricia Thompson, and Sherry Rogers Seibel. Your feedback helped me improve my manuscript for publication.

I also have to thank the people who were early readers of the manuscript and took the time to write testimonials and endorsements for my memoir: Susan Lynch, Kathy Santo, Joe Connor, Tim Brown, and Elena Breese.

To the University of Virginia Law Library, thank you for your assistance with securing the courtroom sketches of the Torres trial by Ida Libby Dengrove.

To the people behind the scenes who helped me with marketing: Linda McHugh, web design; Susan Englert of Bradstreet Englert Creative; and Niki Gallagher-Garcia and Jenn T. Grace from Publish Your Purpose.

The biggest thank you ever to A.Y. Berthiaume, who helped me turn my original mess of a manuscript into a memoir that I am very proud of. It's been a pleasure working with you, and I loved every minute of my writing experience. I share your belief in the healing power of storytelling as I came out of this experience with a better understanding of myself.

I also have to thank Bridgett McGowen-Hawkins and her awesome team at Press 49 for their expertise in guiding me through publishing and improving every one of my ideas.

I will always be grateful to my husband, Bill, who loves me for who I am with my baggage, sarcasm, and multiple dogs. I am so fortunate to have you in my life.

Last but not least, I thank you, my reader, for showing an interest in my story. It's not easy to put your personal story on paper for the world to see, but I'm hopeful you will gain understanding and strength from my experiences.

FURTHER READINGS

Books on Domestic Terrorism, Radical Movements, and Government Response

Berger, Dan, *Outlaws of America: The Weather Underground and the Politics of Solidarity*. (Chico, CA: AK Press, 2006).

This detailed history draws from primary sources and interviews to examine the development of the Weather Underground and its broader role in revolutionary solidarity and activism.

Burrough, Bryan, *Days of Rage: American's Radical Underground, the FBI, and the Forgotten Age of Revolutionary Violence*. (New York: Penguin Books, 2016).

This book is a gripping narrative history of America's underground radical groups from the 1970s, focusing on their explosive tactics, FBI responses, and eventual decline.

Ingber, Jeff with Joe Connor, *Shattered Lives: Overcoming the Fraunces Tavern Terror*. (Cranford, NJ: Jeff Ingber, 2018).

This is a personal and investigative account of the 1975 Fraunces Tavern bombing by the FALN, blending memoir, history, and counterterrorism insight to explore its lasting trauma.

Levitas, Daniel, *The Terrorist Next Door: The Militia Movement and the Radical Right.* (New York: St. Martin's Press, 2002).

This book is a comprehensive exploration of right-wing extremism in America and how militia groups have evolved since the 1990s.

Varon, Jeremy, *Bringing the War Home: The Weather Underground, the Red Army Faction, and Revolutionary Violence in the Sixties and Seventies.* (Berkeley, CA: University of California Press, 2004).

This is an in-depth comparative analysis of leftist revolutionary violence, examining the motivations, philosophies, and tactics of the Weather Underground and Germany's Red Army Faction.

Books on the FALN

Denis, Nelson A., *The War Against All Puerto Ricans: Revolution and Terror in America's Colony.* (New York: Bold Type Books, 2016).

This book provides a comprehensive history of Puerto Rico's struggle for independence, including detailed accounts of the FALN's activities and the U.S. government's response. Denis offers a critical examination of the political and social dynamics that fueled the independence movement.

Jiménez de Wagenheim, Olga, editor, *Puerto Rican Nationalism: A Reader.* (Princeton, NJ: Markus Wiener Publishers, 2016).

This anthology compiles essential writings and speeches from key figures in the Puerto Rican nationalist movement, offering insights into the ideological underpinnings of groups like the FALN. It's a valuable resource for understanding the historical context of their actions.

Torres, Andrés and José E. Velázquez, editors, *The Puerto Rican Movement: Voices from the Diaspora.* (Philadelphia: Temple University Press, 2001).

This collection features essays and interviews with activists involved in the Puerto Rican independence movement in the U.S., including discussions on the FALN. It sheds light on the broader diaspora's role in the struggle for Puerto Rican self-determination.

Velázquez, José E., *Armed Struggle and the Search for State: The FALN and the Puerto Rican Independence Movement.* (Gainsville, FL: University Press of Florida, 2009).

This book interrogates how violence, statehood, and resistance are understood and remembered, raising questions about nationalism, identity, and the ethics of revolutionary activism.

ABOUT THE AUTHOR

Christiane Scarpino is a licensed speech-language pathologist and retired massage therapist who now devotes her life to raising awareness about post-traumatic stress disorder (PTSD). A Rutgers University and Purdue University graduate, she lives in New Jersey with her husband and their cherished Nova Scotia Duck Tolling Retrievers, with whom she trains and competes in various performance events.

A survivor of a terrorist bombing in 1977, Christiane's life took a dramatic turn as she grappled with the long-lasting effects of PTSD. Her memoir, *Missing Pieces*, shares her deeply personal journey of resilience, highlighting the hidden struggles of trauma survivors and the importance of understanding the condition's impact on daily life. Through her story, she provides a powerful message of hope for fellow survivors and advocates for greater awareness, empathy, and support for those living with invisible wounds.

Christiane's mission is to educate others about PTSD, emphasizing the need for accommodations and under-standing—even for those who may appear "normal" on the outside. By sharing her experiences, she aims to inspire trauma survivors and foster a greater sense of compassion and connection in society.

Christiane trains and competes with her dogs in Agility, Obedience, Dock Diving, and Field. She also volunteers at a local shelter as a dog trainer. She is a hunt test judge for the Hunting Retriever Club (HRC) and loves to watch dogs do the jobs they were bred to do. She is an avid hydroponic gardener and grows many vegetables indoors.

www.ingramcontent.com/pod-product-compliance
Lightning Source LLC
Chambersburg PA
CBHW021709120626
46545CB00004B/1468